The DaVinci Method™

"Set your genius on Fire;

And come alive!

Create. Discover. Lead.

The world needs Light.

And you, my friend,

Carry a torch."

Garret LoPorto

The DaVinci Method
Version 1.39

Visit us at www.DaVinciMethod.com

The advice offered in this book, although based on the author's extensive experience and research, is not intended to be a substitute for the advice and counsel of your physician or other health-care providers. Rather, it is intended to offer information to help the reader cooperate with their support community in a mutual quest for optimal well-being.

By continuing to read this book you, the reader, implicitly agree to the following statement:

I understand that the information presented in this book is for educational purposes only. Therefore, if I wish to apply ideas contained in this book, I take full responsibility for my subsequent actions and their results.

*"Don't ask what the world needs.
Ask what makes you come alive,
and go do it.
Because what the world needs
is people who have come alive."*

~ Howard Thurman
[American clergy, civil rights activist & mystic]

*"Men of genius
are meteors intended to burn
to light their century."*

~ Napoleon Bonaparte

About the Author

Garret LoPorto, writer, speaker, U.S. & International patent-pending inventor, and successful entrepreneur who has been written about in The New York Times, Money Magazine, The London Financial Times, The Boston Globe and many other newspapers. He and his projects have also been featured on national television, including CNN and ABC, and on Nitebeat, MIT TV and New England Cable News.

He was the founder and CEO of a multi-million dollar technology & media company. He has worked in Microsoft Research – a prestigious think tank where some of the most gifted thinkers perform advanced work in computer sciences.

He has lectured at such venues as MIT, The University of Massachusetts and The Computer Freedom and Privacy Convention.

He lives in Concord, Massachusetts with his wife, Heather, and their children.

To book Garret LoPorto for your event or interview, please call 800-827-1230 or email **info@davincimethod.com** .

To my son, John.

Acknowledgments

Thank you, John for being my greatest teacher and the one guy who can show me my deepest faults and my most tender wounds. You are the one who has shown me the way.

Thank you, Heather for being my inspiration, the yin to my yang, and my best friend. Thank you for helping me make this book happen. If it weren't for your kindness, your patience, your belief in me, your tireless listening, and your editing of this book, The DaVinci Method may have never been finished.

Thank you, Marty Sussman for being such a good friend and mentor. You helped me open doors I couldn't find the courage or the strength to open myself. You were generous with me when you didn't need to be and you helped me find the will to do this work. You were the one who told me "You gotta do this!" regarding writing The DaVinci Method – albeit in a dream, (so now I may be thanking you for something my unconscious actually did, but you filled the archetype wonderfully).

Thank you, Ava for being a most delightful distraction. Your charming beauty and sparkle have almost rendered this book impossible. Your 2 AM & 5 AM wake-ups made me a vegetable for 9 months. It is rare to find someone so captivating and endearing that one is willing to lose everything for another moment in her presence. You my dear – along with your beautiful mother – are that someone for me.

Thank you, Ben Cohen for being a great role-model. Your insistence that I always ask the question "what for?" before embarking on a mission has saved me many useless journeys. Thank you, Andrew Greenblatt for being like a big brother to me. Thank you Duane Peterson, for always looking out for me and getting me involved.

Thank you, Russell Bishop for being a great teacher. Your honesty, impeccability, and inner-trust have inspired me.

Thank you, Valerie Bishop for being there just when I would need a word of wisdom.

Thank you, Thom Hartmann for having such a striking sensibility in our talk over nachos with Marianne in DC. You helped me to discover your thoughtful work, through which I remembered my own. Your work is one of the proverbial giants whose shoulders this work stands upon.

Thank you Marianne Williamson for welcoming me into your life with such faith, showing me what the author's life is really like and encouraging me to become one myself.

Thank you to Otto Rank for developing the most amazing therapy, sadly forgotten by history, but joyfully resurrected here.

Thank you, Dave LoVecchio for reminding me of the "rats in the basement."

Thank you, Mom and Dad for your editing suggestions and for introducing me to the world that has influenced much of the writing of this book.

Thank you, Captain John for being my hero.

CONTENTS

Answering the Call ...

Once upon a time an eagle's egg was found by a farmer and mistaken for a chicken egg. The egg was placed with the other eggs in the incubator at the hen house.

Some weeks later that egg hatched. The baby eagle was born and raised as a chicken with his chicken peers. He was taught to peck and scratch. He was taught to scurry along the ground like the other chickens. He was sternly warned against flying, because chickens don't really fly, they flutter and fall.

This eagle made a miserable chicken. He didn't scurry well. He didn't peck well. He was always hungry, because the chicken feed just wasn't satisfying to him. The other chickens found him disruptive.

After years of struggling to be a normal chicken, this poor eagle's self esteem was pretty low. He hated himself. "Why am I so big, and awkward and unusual looking?" he would wonder, "Why can I not find satisfaction in those things that satisfy all the other chickens?"

"Is this all there is to life?" he agonized, "Where's the thrill and excitement?!"

He began to do more and more disruptive things just to get a little hit of excitement. He was starved for action and adventure, so he tried to make up his own thrilling dramas around the chicken coop. Other chickens caught on to his discontent and called him selfish, disordered and a troublemaker. The poor eagle took it all to heart and became depressed.

One day, high overhead the young eagle saw another eagle soaring high in the sky. It took his breath away. For that moment he felt a surge of recognition. He felt something inside him stirring and he felt more alive than he ever had.

In his excitement he told his family of chickens what he saw and they scoffed at him. "Flying is risky, irresponsible and impractical." the chickens warned. "When will you grow up and join the pecking order of this chicken coop. Why can't you be more like your peers?"

The young eagle was shamed and disheartened. He felt hopeless and alone as he fell to sleep that night.

The next day, to his delight, he spotted that same eagle soaring up above. And this time the soaring bird let out the cry of an eagle.

The moment the young eagle heard this cry something unexpected happened. The young eagle raised by chickens found his body lurching and his throat contracting. Uncontrollably his entire being responded to that eagle's cry with his own majestic eagle cry.

He was astonished. "What had just happened?" "Did that glorious sound come from him? Chickens don't make that sound! Only eagles do. … Wait. … Only eagles do!"

The young eagle, finally aware of what he truly was, stretched out his wings for the first time and flew. He was no longer imprisoned by the chicken coop, because he was no longer imprisoned by the idea that he had to be a chicken. Nothing could contain him anymore.

A chicken coop can only coop chickens; it cannot stop an eagle from soaring when he hears his call.

Have you heard *your* call?

Maybe this is it.

What is a DaVinci?

DaVincis are the change-agents of society. DaVincis are the world's greatest leaders, artists, entrepreneurs, inventors, revolutionaries and rock stars. DaVincis are the ones who know first, who sense earliest the disturbances in the fabric of human affairs – the trends, the patterns, the fashions, the revolutions that are afoot, the coming groundswells of popular demand.

DaVincis are light bearers and leaders. They are the proverbial canaries in the mineshaft. DaVincis are often the most sensitive of our population, the most creative, and potentially the most destructive.

DaVincis share a common genetic polymorphism, the DRD4 exon III 7-repeat allele. This gene supports risk-taking, novelty seeking, increased alpha/theta brainwave patterns, susceptibility to addictive behavior, ADD/ADHD and bipolar, propensity for genius level problem solving and creativity, and gives one what it takes to be a charismatic political leader, rock star, inventor, movie-maker, artist or rebel billionaire.

DaVincis have very little natural self-repression. Where the vast majority of the population may be quite repressed and content with that, the mere 10% of the population who are DaVinci types abhor any inner self-repression. DaVincis are only really content when operating at 100% threshold of their physical, mental, emotional and spiritual capacity with virtually no self–repression holding them back.

Where an average citizen is happy living at about 30% of their natural capacity, DaVincis are only happy when they are throwing their entire being, 100%, into each situation holding nothing back at all.

Since lack of self-repression is often perceived to be socially unacceptable, DaVincis may develop the maladaptive approach of holding everything back until there is a crisis – a socially acceptable excuse to throw 100% of themselves into that situation – as a result DaVincis often find or generate crisis after crisis in order to feel fully engaged, happy and alive.

Another maladaptive response to the social norms of repression is to "shut down." Many DaVincis preempt negative feedback from their community (for being too spontaneous, impulsive, unexpected, uncontrolled and "different") by preemptively subjugating their own irrepressible nature with a veneer of inauthentic behavioral repression.

The difference between the self-repression experienced by the other 90% of the population and the behavioral repression experienced by frustrated DaVincis, is that regular self-repression stops unconscious ideas, impulses, thoughts and desires from reaching consciousness – while behavioral repression leaves a person fully exposed consciously or semi-consciously to this storm of unconscious ideas, impulses, thoughts and desires, while nothing but the brute force of their conscious ego is left to stop their wild nature from being acted out in the world through their behavior.

A person who is a DaVinci type and is also behaviorally repressed often appears stiff, unnatural, emotionally dishonest, stunted, all-bottled-up, frustrated, anal retentive and even constipated. That is because they are straining to hold back the rush of unconscious ideas and impulses that fill their consciousness in order to avoid expressing something that would be deemed "inappropriate" by their community.

The other 90% of the population called the Normal types, seem to have it easy, because they are generally unaware of all the unconscious material that their brains automatically repress without any conscious effort. So in effect, they have relatively little conflict between what they experience consciously and what can act out behaviorally. Because Normal types rarely ever experience their unconscious ideas, impulses, thoughts and desires consciously, they don't have to actively block anything, so they appear normal and natural, albeit lacking much flare, creativity and fire.

The behaviorally repressed DaVinci type can suffer greatly from hypomania, anxiety, bipolar disorder, depression, ADD, ADHD, addiction, compulsiveness, procrastination, dishonesty and lack of true success.

Sigmund Freud's most creative protégé, Otto Rank, spent his career studying the special case of DaVinci psychology – what he once called the psychology of the artist. Rank called the DaVinci type who is stuck in behavioral repression "the neurotic." He later went on to develop a complete therapy for the neurotic DaVinci type, which helps one to become the productive DaVinci type or "the Artist". His work was brilliant and effective, but alas, it has been mostly forgotten by history because his therapy only was applicable to about 10% of the general population whom are DaVincis.

Almost 100 years later we live in a culture rich in medical diagnosis and we have labeled many of the neurotic DaVinci types ADD or ADHD. Even productive DaVincis often jokingly describe themselves as having ADD.

Now that the world is finally ready for it, we are glad to offer Rank's revolutionary therapy back to the world. This updated therapy – combined with the powerful recent discoveries in EEG brainwave measurement– will help you discover your greatest potential and *live it*.

(EEG Brainwave measurement has revealed the special properties of how a DaVinci type's brain works and how food, drugs, sports, exercise, sex and even honesty (versus deception) uniquely affect a DaVinci's brain.)

If you see a bit of the neurotic DaVinci type in you, take heart. Through The DaVinci Method you can transform yourself from a neurotic DaVinci type into the great productive DaVinci type ("the Artist") that you were meant to be.

A Word on "Indigo Children"

If you're reading this book looking for helpful information about Indigo children, please note that we'll be referring to them as Theta DaVinci types. You will probably find the second half of this book particularly helpful and inspiring.

The Addictive Personality

Virtually all DaVincis could be said to have "addictive personalities." In fact, when someone refers to an addictive personality, they are usually referring to a DaVinci.

DaVincis are impulsive sensation-seekers and natural-born risk takers. DaVincis crave that ecstatic high – that larger than life experience – that rush that comes from living on the edge, challenging the status quo and doing something new.

When DaVincis don't reach that ecstatic experience in their day-to-day lives they soon find surrogates to artificially create that experience, or find self-destructive ways to suppress their desire for it. Later in this book, we'll show you a revolutionary approach to dealing with the common DaVinci problems of addiction and compulsion in a way that transforms these addictive compulsions back into the miraculous creative impulses they originate as.

Before delving into this subject it is often most helpful to first understand the DaVinci personality more thoroughly. Though, you *can* skip ahead to the section "Transcending Addiction" if you must.

A Word on Disorders (ADD/ADHD, bipolar & More)

Let us be clear right from the beginning. The DaVinci trait is a great thing, but our society has not traditionally honored those with this gift. Because 9 out of 10 people *do not* have the DaVinci trait, popular opinion and culture tends to be intolerant of the DaVinci temperament and the DaVincis' general approach to life.

This intolerance comes in many forms, most of them subtle. The general structure of our society is geared towards catering to the interests of and rewarding the qualities of the Normal type.

Most Normal types thrive on feelings of "safety" and find comfort in the structured confines of laws, rules, tradition, hierarchies, and establishment, because the Normal type is risk averse and has a low tolerance for change. So our institutions, our schools; and our legal system reward those who follow the rules and don't challenge authority; but that is not the way of DaVincis.

DaVincis think differently, (or as the DaVincis at Apple Computer say "Think different."). DaVincis constantly challenge the norm, question authority and work outside of the rules. DaVincis do this because they are brilliant out-of-the-box thinkers. DaVincis sense the problems and inadequacies of the hierarchies that they find themselves in; and take it into their own hands to solve them.

Even at a young age DaVinci children sense the lack of genuine intimacy in their communities, feel the void of spontaneous expression from others and begin to see the lack of true honesty and integrity from the authority figures in their lives. DaVincis learn quite early on that society and authority cannot be trusted with their deepest sensitivities, their honest insights and their truest impulses.

Generally our culture condemns or shames unexpected or extreme ideas and behaviors because these ideas and behaviors often threaten the established power structure – or, at very least, reveal how little control the established structure really has.

DaVincis are full of spontaneous and unexpected ideas and behavior. So, as you might expect, DaVincis are generally condemned or shamed for their new approaches or spontaneous actions – no matter how right they might actually be. If this condemnation and shaming is internalized by a DaVinci child it generally leads to one of a myriad of personality or behavioral disorders.

One of the most common disorders developed is ADD/ADHD. Some others of note are depression, bipolar disorder, narcissism, anxiety, oppositional defiance disorder, and addiction – but all of them seem to lead back to the root cause of a frustrated DaVinci temperament. That does not mean that if you have the DaVinci trait, you must develop a disorder. But chances are if, in your formative years, you were exposed to environments hostile to your DaVinci temperament you probably have developed at least some traces of what Otto Rank called "neurotic tendencies" or what today is commonly called a "disorder".

So ADD/ADHD, bipolar and these other disorders are basically the negative expression of the DaVinci temperament. Hyperactivity, depression and over-distractibility are generally the symptoms of frustrated and out of balance DaVincis. If you are a DaVinci and you have not cultivated yourself in a way that is compatible with your natural DaVinci temperament, you will most likely have developed ADD/ADHD, depression or bipolar. This is curable.

These disorders are the result of not working to your strengths when you have the DaVinci trait. ADD/ADHD and bipolar are the other edge of the DaVinci gene's double edged sword. With the DaVinci gene you will either be "in the flow" with your God-given brilliance or you will be struggling to fit in – trying to be like the other 90% of the population called "normal". *You are not normal.*

You have a choice, let go and be brilliant with grace and ease, or struggle your whole life just to be mediocre. ADD/ADHD and depression are the direct result and symptoms of rejecting your brilliance. ADD/ADHD and depression come from forcing yourself to behave in artificial ways, (often fueled by your desire to "fit in"), instead of just letting go of "shoulds" and just being you.

You can ignore your genius, you can fight your truest nature, you can try to fit in behaviorally, but in the end, if you have the activated DaVinci gene, all this will do is frustrate you and make you disordered.

You – with the activated DaVinci gene – basically have a choice: Be brilliant or suffer from the symptoms of ADD/ADHD along with the potential to develop many other disorders like depression, addiction, narcissism, anxiety, obsessive compulsive disorder, and bi-polar disorder.

For the rest of this book we will refer to the dark side of the DaVinci trait expression, which includes ADD/ADHD symptoms along with all those other issues, as "the neurotic type." The positive expression of the DaVinci trait will be called "the Artist."

"The Artist" will be used throughout this work to describe the creative and productive expression available to all DaVincis. This expression could also aptly be called "the genius" or be expressed in the frame of other creative/productive endeavors where DaVincis become brilliant such as "the entrepreneur," "the inventor," "the leader," "the evangelist," "the athlete," "the rock star," "the warrior," "the explorer," "the general," "the mystic," "the hero," "the healer," etcetera.

You'll note "the best of the best" in all of the above pursuits are fully equipped with the DaVinci temperament and in their worse moments express symptoms of the many disorders listed above, including ADHD and bipolar disorder.

Are You A DaVinci?

"Thousands of geniuses live and die undiscovered
– either by themselves or by others."
~ Mark Twain

Take the DaVinci test:

► Do you often try new things just for fun or thrills?

► Do you often do things based on how you feel in the moment without worrying about how it was done in the past?

► Are you a jack of all trades? Do you feel more capable than most in adapting yourself to new situations, solving unexpected problems, and learning new tasks?

► Do you have trouble wrapping up the final details of a project, once the interesting & challenging problems have been solved?

► When you have a task that requires a lot of thought, do you avoid or delay getting started?

► Do you feel compelled to overdo things just to feel more awake or alive or safe?

► Do you have difficulty staying organized?

► Do you often feel half-asleep while going about your routine tasks?

► Do you crave adventure, new experiences and/or new ideas?

► Do you have a short attention span – that is, unless a particular subject has captured your imagination?

▶ Do you act impulsively or dangerously more often than the average citizen?

▶ Do you have a tendency to allow your mind to drift away from boring conversation?

▶ Do you have a tendency toward compulsive behavior?

▶ Do you have difficulty feeling fully awake?

▶ Do you have broad mood swings from very high to very low?

▶ Do you frequently daydream or "space out" when you are not at the center of the action?

If you answered "yes" to 10 or more of these questions, congratulations! You are most likely a DaVinci and a member of a rare and powerful genetic group (that encompasses less than 10% of the global population).

See a movie about what it means to be a DaVinci and try the online DaVinci test at: **www.AreYouaDaVinci.com**

Who was Leonardo da Vinci?

"The most heavenly gifts seem to be showered on
certain human beings. Sometimes supernaturally,
marvelously, they all congregate in one individual.
… This was seen and acknowledged by all men in
the case of Leonardo da Vinci, who had . . . an
indescribable grace in every effortless act and deed.
His talent was so rare that he mastered any subject
to which he turned his attention."

~ Giorgio Vasari

Leonardo da Vinci was the epitome of the Renaissance Man. da Vinci's *The Last Supper* (1495-97) and *The Mona Lisa* (1503-06) are among the most widely popular and influential paintings of the Renaissance. His notebooks reveal a spirit of scientific inquiry and a mechanical inventiveness that were centuries ahead of his time.

Da Vinci mastered many disciplines easily. He forged new paths of exploration. He created great works of art and beauty. He designed machines that captured the imagination. He was an artist, an inventor, an architect, a musician, an engineer and a leader. He was the closest thing to a creative entrepreneur for his time.

Much of Leonardo's work was left unfinished. He was infamous for his unwillingness to complete many of his commissioned projects. Be it that a project lost its challenge for him or he discovered some greater project along the way that more fully captured his attention, da Vinci went wherever his passion led him in the moment.

Leonardo DaVinci was an extreme example of the best and worst parts of what we have been calling the DaVinci trait. He was brilliant, yet he didn't finish much of what he started. Sometimes his choice to abandon one project for another was a wise exercise of intuition, sensing it was time to move on. Other times he simply couldn't finish a work due to his fear of completion. These incompletions he later regretted on his death-bed.

Otto Rank taught us that DaVincis experience every aspect of life as a whole instead of in parts like the Normal type do. So, major completions can seem as scary as meeting death for a DaVinci, because it is experienced as an ending of everything. This is also an element of what is sometimes called hyperfocus. We will discuss this in more detail later.

What does Leonardo da Vinci represent?

Leonardo glorified the Renaissance humanist ideal …

"Humanism teaches us that it is immoral to wait for God to act for us. We must act to stop the wars and the crimes and the brutality of this and future ages. We have powers of a remarkable kind. We have a high degree of freedom in choosing what we will do. Humanism tells us that whatever our philosophy of the universe may be, ultimately the responsibility for the kind of world in which we live rests with us."

~ Minister Kenneth Phifer

Da Vinci was an example of your limitless potential. He was one of the most ruthlessly honest people of all time. He was unafraid of discovery – of peering into the depths of the human condition and even the dark unexplored territory of human anatomy – in order to better mankind's plight. His honesty allowed him to look where others never dared.

Through his honesty and his genetically predisposed ability to access his unconscious mind consciously, DaVinci was able to dream in entirely new paradigms for art, science, engineering and mankind.

Leonardo da Vinci also had his struggles. He failed to complete much of what he started. He regretted having "wasted" much of his life. Leonardo was subject to the same frailties as we all are and he did not have a manual like this one to help him manage his temperament more consistently.

The DaVinci Revolution –

Leonardo da Vinci's Messages

Leonardo's notebooks and masterpieces have left us with much to ponder. The genius and the intricacies of his inventions are still being discovered to the astonishment of scientists today. But let us not be lost in a materialist perception of his work for there are deeper spiritual messages available.

The message of Leonardo's mysterious painting – The Last Supper – may be that Christianity and Western thought at the time had forgotten the power of Eros in its doctrine. That without Eros, Logos – the mental, masculine externalized approach to spirituality – is too literal and externally focused to reach the inner truth it was intended to help one reach.

Think of Eros and Logos as the Feminine & Masculine counterparts of God. God's place in our existence is often a parental figure in theology. This could be thought of as Mom and Dad – Mother Earth in union with God the Father. In a traditional sense, Mom feeds you and cares for your physical health in a tactile way. Dad *talks* to you, passes his wisdom to you, passes his wealth to you; he's the voice of authority.

Eros - interrelational, tactile, sensory and sensual. Logos - ordering, masterful, problem-solving, rule-making, verbal and heady.

Thus a Christianity relying solely on Logos, on external rules of conduct, authority and intellectualism is missing half the picture. True divinity has both Logos and Eros. True genius is both intellectually & outwardly relevant and is also receptive to deep intuition. Both masculine assertiveness & feminine receptivity working together makes the 'total human'– often called the "mystic" or the "genius". This is what Leonardo da Vinci personified.

The DaVinci Method is devoted to helping you discover for yourself that perfect balance point of consciousness between your inner and outer worlds and, in so doing, will help you discover your inner ability to sense the "ring of truth" which carries with it more power than you realize.

The Ring of Truth

As you read The DaVinci Method, you may be surprised by how many statements simply ring true for you. When this happens, don't second guess yourself. Trust that sense of rightness.

We live in culture so saturated with the external authority of mass media that we have become afraid of our own intuition. You can know something – and be right – long before there is ever solid agreement of it. You can know beauty and love, inspiration and truth without corroboration. You just know it, because it is.

This is the way of the leader, the artist, the entrepreneur and the pioneer. Every great discoverer "knows" his destination before it is realized. It is the trust in his own inner-knowing that makes his discoveries possible.

So as you read The DaVinci Method when something rings true, trust that ring of truth – and try it. If when you try it, it works, then trust that experience – and use it.

Your DaVinci Gene

Your Secret DRD4 Difference

Ten percent of the world population has a mysterious genetic polymorphism that originated thousands of years ago – this polymorphism appears to be the key to being a DaVinci. The polymorphism is actually an elongation of the DRD4-exon III gene. People who carry this gene and whose environments have activated it display a novelty seeking, thrill-seeking, more impulsive temperament that is radically less inhibited and much more powerfully connected to deep spontaneous intuition.

"The long repeats of the DRD4-exon III polymorphism are related to Novelty Seeking personality trait."

~ AMERICAN JOURNAL OF MEDICAL GENETICS[1]

This gene has been positively selected over the millennia since this variation first appeared. Experts have speculated that it is because the traits this gene engenders serves one well in the heat of battle, in hunting, in innovation and exploration.

"A gene associated with novelty-seeking and attention deficit hyperactivity disorder, DRD4, has also been shown to have undergone recent positive selection.[2]"

~ Human Molecular Genetics[3]

The people who carry the elongated repeats of DRD4-exon III polymorphism can truthfully be called carriers of the latest genetic evolution impacting human consciousness. They are the new warriors, discoverers, conquerors, artists and mystics.

Your DRD4 gene is a key player in the way your brain regulates dopamine, which is the neurotransmitter responsible for your sensitivity to sensory stimulation. If your brain has more dopamine receptors (or less dopamine) than someone else's brain you will tend to seek out more sensory stimulation than them.

Richard P. Ebstein published in the journal *Nature Genetics* that he and his colleagues at Herzog Memorial Hospital and Ben-Gurion University in Israel found that "people tend to be extroverted, impulsive, extravagant, quick-tempered, excitable and exploratory" who have the DRD4-exon III repeats variation.

In the United States at the National Institutes of Health, Dean Hamer and Jonathan Benjamin published in the journal *Nature Genetics* their finding that "Those who scored highest in novelty-seeking, impulsive, quick-tempered, and fickle were most likely to have long repeats of DNA subunits in their D4 dopamine receptor gene."

DRD4 may not be the only genetic source of these qualities, it may be part of a group of genes working together and DRD4 may be just the first to be well charted. Other genes influencing the expression of the DRD4 polymorphisms could result in the variations of the DaVinci trait we observe.

The bottom line is that this genetic difference that makes up the DaVinci trait has a significant impact on your brain's relationship with dopamine. This new relationship makes you particularly well adapted to rapidly changing, intense situations. It makes your brain crave more stimulation and that thrilling sensation of risk than the average person.

The Normal type can survive emergencies when given time to think; and they can do okay tactically in rapidly changing, intense situations when they rely on their primal instinct, but the normal human primal instincts do not offer much grace in fast situations. Primal instincts are based on the immediate innate biological survival mechanisms called "fight or flight". They don't offer much in the way of creativity or problem solving, but primal instincts will get you to drop everything and run away from danger.

The DaVinci type (or 'total human' as Otto Rank called them) is wired differently. The DaVinci DRD4 polymorphism makes the brain crave risk, action and adventure. So it takes a lot more situational intensity to throw a DaVinci into a "fight or flight" primal instinct state. When confronted with the kinds of negotiable dangers that would ordinarily throw a Normal type into the primal fight or flight state, DaVincis will often feel exhilarated, more alive and lucid. Instead of causing terror, the action puts the DaVinci into what's called a high Alpha state that is often described by great athletes as "the zone". From this place gestalts of intuition will flow and will provide the DaVinci with graceful solutions that transcend anything primal instincts could offer. The DaVinci has overcome victimhood and become a lucid player in the dance with danger.

This Alpha or flow state opens the door to one's unconscious mind and thus gives a DaVinci access to a third option besides primal instinct and intellectual planning – the sixth sense. This sixth sense is an unexplainable gestalt of everything one has ever sensed consciously or unconsciously. It is experienced as a clear and vibrant impulse towards a particular solution. Some people call it "a hunch."

In rapidly changing, intense situations that call for immediate action the DaVinci will just "know" what to do and the outcome of that knowing is nothing short of miraculous. This sixth sense does not come through primal survival instincts that are fast but strategically narrow or through intellectual strategic thinking that is far too slow to be useful in "hot" situations. The DaVinci sixth sense is an instant evolution of everything in one's mind into a perfect key, delivered lightening fast, as a flash of insight at the perfect moment. It's like being thrown a sword, in the heat of battle, just in the knick of time.

If this DaVinci trait is so great why is it so rare?

The truth is that while the DaVinci trait yields amazing capabilities, too many DaVincis would get in the way of any mass mobilization towards centralization of power. The old adage "We've got too many chiefs and not enough Indians" comes to mind.

DaVincis are inherently mavericks, rebels and loose cannons. They don't follow rules well and they are often disruptive to large hierarchical human structures. Over the course of history many powerful civilizations have been built by instituting laws and structures that appeal to the Normal types. Being part of a vast hierarchal worker class is actually quite satisfying to the temperament of the Normal type. However, trying to organize DaVincis this way is like herding cats. DaVincis hate being told what to do by outer authorities; Normal types love it.

DaVinci type brains operate from a different center than that of Normal types. Normal type brains are well wired to operate from the more task oriented and superficial levels of consciousness where conditioning, rules, objectives, social norms, laws and conformity register most prominently in awareness. This is the level of consciousness where childhood conditioning is most powerful and tends to be a dominant thought and behavior.

DaVinci types tend to operate from a level of consciousness that is more fluid, less regimented and less easily influenced by parental, cultural and social programming. This level of consciousness does not hold onto outer directives as forcefully, and thus leaves plenty of room for improvisation.

The benefit of Normal types to large conquering empires is that a Normal type child can be easily programmed from a young age with rules of conduct that they will tend to follow unquestioningly for the rest of their lives. This propensity makes building vast civilizations, using Normal types as predictable building blocks, much easier than endlessly trying to convince every maverick DaVinci to go along with a master plan.

The rarer DaVincis are in a given population, the easier that population is to rule. When human civilizations have needed large populations of easily programmed and compliant worker classes, then the Normal type was naturally selected – probably in large part because DaVinci non-conformists would have been ostracized or killed by the ruling class before they could pass on any more of their non-conformist DaVinci genes.

Is DRD4 Activated?

This DRD4 polymorphism, like many other genetic traits, might need to be activated to lead to the DaVinci trait. That means one could be a "carrier" of this special version of the DRD4 gene without actually exhibiting any of the DaVinci trait qualities. Often high stress situations activate genes best equipped to help one handle those situations.

> *"We are studying how cells adapt to*
> *environmental-stress to survive.*
> *In order to survive under stress,*
> *cells activate multiple genes."*

~ SHINOHARA, Toshimichi, Ph.D.
Brigham and Women's Hospital
Center for Ophthalmic Research

Those of us who have the activated DaVinci trait, have likely undergone some form of stress regarded by our bodies as life-threatening and requiring greater volition and ability in typically fight-or-flight situations.

Even something as simple as sleep apnea can cause ADD/ADHD symptoms. These symptoms indicate that one's

DaVinci gene has been activated. Sleep apnea as experienced by the body is equivalent to asphyxiation in the night, so that's clearly another form of stress that would be regarded by the body as life-threatening.

Once our DaVinci trait is activated I don't believe it's something we can deactivate. I think it becomes permanently expressed in us.

And so once it's expressed in us we find we feel a need for stimulation, we feel a need for excitement, for thrills, for adrenaline, for exploring and discovering and doing things differently, because now we're wired differently. Now we crave that transcendent experience of "living on the edge" and being in "the zone".

Thrill-seekers

"There's nothing so exhilarating as being shot at without result."

~ Winston Churchill

Many scientists call this DaVinci DRD4 polymorphism "the thrill-seeking gene." If you love action and adventure a bit more than most people, then chances are you have this gene.

It is easy to see that people with blue eyes must have the 'blue eyes' gene without actually having to test for it. (Incidentally that gene is EYCL3 (also called bey2), which is the brown/blue eye color gene located on chromosome 15.) It is equally easy to spot the DaVinci temperament by its telltale qualities of persistent impulsivity, risk-taking, thrill-seeking and distractibility. You can gather that someone who has this temperament probably has the DRD4 "thrill seeking gene" that scientists have recently discovered.

While people can wear color contacts and exhibit blue eyes without having the gene for blue eyes; people can exhibit DaVinci qualities like distractibility and impulsiveness without actually having the DRD4 DaVinci gene. The key difference is that true DaVincis will be hard-wired to have abundant energy, creativity and the genuine desire for risk and adventure all of the time – even when taken out of the kinds of modern, over-stimulating environments that might cause a Normal type to exhibit those qualities.

People who are naturally attracted to becoming police officers, firemen, warriors and generals usually have this thrill seeking DaVinci gene. These are the type of people who really feel more alive when in the epicenter of a crisis.

To prefer chasing someone down in your police car or racing, at the drop of a hat, to a fire you're going to just throw your body into – to prefer all that intensity to a comfortable air-conditioned desk job – that's something special.

The type of people who are attracted to these experiences are the same type of people who have this activated DRD4 thrill seeking, novelty seeking, impulsivity gene.

> *"Genetically there seems to be no doubt that the Kennedy's must carry what many scientists refer to as the 'thrill seeking gene'"*
>
> ~ Edward Klein
> [author of the book The Kennedy Curse]

After 9/11 there was an almost symbolic awakening to the value of "the hero." We're moving into an age now where those who do have the activated DRD4 gene are once again acknowledged as being a precious human resource, because they are the ones who will risk everything, giving their lives to rescue humanity from the violence of cold rationality. They bring balance and heart back to our overly mechanized lives.

DaVincis would rather usher in a new Renaissance as opposed to allowing the status-quo to continue. The chaotically imbalanced environment we currently find ourselves in will likely be replaced with a new order only a DaVinci could conceive.

If enough of us who have this DRD4 polymorphism activation can just honor our impulsive brilliance and nurture our desire to create beauty and innovate, collectively we can usher in a new era of genuine beauty and creativity – a neo-Renaissance – which can replace old structures with new vitality and heart.

The Irrepressible DaVinci

DaVinci types have far less natural repression than Normal types. Repression appears to be engendered by the fear of reality. DaVinci types, being thrill seekers, enjoy the rush of facing the uncontrollable nature of reality and riding it like a wave. They do not fear the unknown as much as they welcome it.

The highly repressed make poor surfers and thus avoid surfing at all costs. The DaVincis can't help but surf the wild impulses of their powerful unconscious, for doing so is in their very nature. And, with a little practice, they can become quite good at it.

The great artists, inventors, entrepreneurs and leaders of our day are great surfers of their unconscious minds. They may not describe it that way, but that's precisely what they are doing when they are making their most powerful choices.

"True genius resides in the capacity for evaluation of uncertain, hazardous, and conflicting information."

~ Winston Churchill

A Neo-Renaissance?

Five hundred years ago a revolution of human thought and potential took place. The entire human race was elevated by an elect group of savant saviors who took it upon themselves to raise the masses from the pits of chaos into a new order.

That time has come and gone. Now we find ourselves once again in a collective chaos, and a herald has been sounded for those who will elect to transform themselves and the world from the inside out. It is your calling to usher in a new era and a new order to replace the last, for you are beginning a journey walking in the genes of the great DaVinci.

Five hundred years ago the world wasn't as connected as it is now. Communication was slower, so the world was made up of what seemed like many smaller worlds all isolated from one another. What happened in one part of Europe didn't immediately and directly seem to affect other parts of Europe at the time. There were different pockets of culture and society.

Consider that there were two parallel worlds, in Europe alone. One world existed in Italy where there was a lot of strife and a lot of bloodshed. There were many feudal powers struggling for control of the lands and the proletariat. This was around the time when Machiavelli wrote The Prince. The Prince details how one can effectively conquer and control people in this violent climate. It is also considered one of the most influential books of all time. The Prince epitomizes the fearful struggle for control so pervasive at this moment in history.

Italy was full of many warlords wrestling for political and military control. Such a chaotic, hectic environment is replete with uncertainty.

Surprisingly, all that discord sparked the inspired beauty of the Renaissance artists, Michelangelo, Leonardo da Vinci, and Rafael. All of these great creators and thinkers came out of this horrendous chaos.

Now, at the same time in Switzerland, things were rather peaceful in comparison. There wasn't a whole lot of upheaval going on. There was a period of tranquility in Switzerland for a long time. And if we compare that to the period of great uncertainty, chaos and bedlam in Italy we'll discover something fascinating. The chaos in Italy prompted its people to become great thinkers and creators.

To create the Renaissance did not take just one brilliant mind – it took many. The Renaissance was a light shed of brilliant minds come alive – and all out of a time of horrible struggle.

On the other hand a virtual utopia has existed in Switzerland. There were many years of nothing happening at all – at least nothing really upsetting on a societal scale. During that period of tranquility the Swiss came out with Swiss cheese and the coo-coo-clock. Relative peace and tranquility does not engender much motivation to innovate.

The old saying that "Necessity is the mother of invention" could be extended into "Disturbances are the mother of genius." The speck of sand in an oyster that becomes the pearl is like the moment of peril in a DaVinci's life that transforms him into a genius.

Walk a Mile in Leonardo da Vinci's Genes.

Leonardo da Vinci lived towards the beginning of the Renaissance. The environment in which he grew up was full of strife. He was the bastard son of a common woman and a "noble" father. His country was overrun with warring feudal states. His step-mothers were not kind to him because he was regarded as a threat to their inheritance; and his formative years were treacherous at best.

This was an all too common situation at the time. Times of intense stress were a hallmark of the pre-Renaissance. It could be argued that the Renaissance was an answer to these highly stressed dark ages – initiated when the collective stress levels reached a critical point. It is precisely this strife filled and stressful upbringing that probably sparked the genetic activation of the DaVinci DRD4 polymorphism in Leonardo da Vinci and many of his brilliant contemporaries.

The Renaissance had its own chaos, and today we have chaos fueled by rapid-fire telecommunications, information overload and mass media. The Renaissance may have activated this DRD4 gene in many and now our present day environment may be doing the same.

The New World Disorder

So now it seems our society has coined a "disorder" to describe the DaVinci trait – ADD/ADHD. We are medicating children with the DaVinci trait with Ritalin to make them more docile and controllable – less rebellious.

Now schools are under the pressure of the President Bush's "No Child Left Behind Act" (Jan 8th, 2002) to push students through rigid curriculums and testing. This can only further encourage the over-propensity to get "troublemakers" (which are usually the more creative DaVinci type students) on Ritalin or Adderall in order to make them more "normal," attentive and more manageable. These drugged DaVinci kids are more manageable because Ritalin literally suppresses the brainwave-states that allow for genius levels of creativity. There will be more on this in the chapters on brainwaves.

Brilliant DaVinci children are often pressured – either with drugs or discipline – into behaving like just another cog in the wheel. We are destroying the confidence of the very children who offer the greatest genius, and then putting them on drugs that suppress their brilliant creativity.

Maybe you've got adult ADD/ADHD or your children are diagnosed as ADD/ADHD. It used to be called LD for Learning Disabled, but now ADD/ADHD has become the label of choice.

> *"Even Leonardo da Vinci would be labeled L.D.*
> *today ... and that's not just because those are his*
> *initials."*

~ Garret LoPorto

More and more medications are springing up to profit from this new groundswell. The pharmaceutical companies are cashing in on this and they have little regard for the long-term consequences of medicating a whole generation of potential geniuses.

This is really symptomatic of our society and our culture. Our environment is in disarray. There is just so much information overload, such constant upheaval.

Granted we have somewhat stable governments in most of the bigger countries, but it's not governments anymore that control our lives so much as the corporations that affect our lives the most. These corporations are just manipulating us, because we are naïve.

Nowadays corporations really have more of the role that feudal states once had back 500 years ago. One way to illustrate this is to look at what entities had the power during each time period, by looking at what entities had the largest, most ornate, expensive structures built in their honor.

If we look at civilizations of about 2,000 – 3,000 years ago, the Greek and Roman Empires were the most powerful. So at that point in time these governments possessed the greatest power and it is the huge government commissioned buildings (like the Roman coliseum) that still stand (albeit in ruins) today.

Then if we look at the largest, most ornate buildings built about a thousand years ago, we'll notice that they're mostly cathedrals and church buildings, because that was when the Catholic Church began to have the most power.

These large structures were the product and evidence of massive centralized wealth gathering.

Finally, nowadays when we just walk in a modern city we know the biggest building is probably owned by a credit card corporation.

So perhaps we're really not so much under the control of our governments. We're much more under the dominion of the large corporations, multi-national corporations – especially banks and credit card companies.

What is interesting about corporations today is with all the mergers and acquisitions going on, corporations lack stable leadership. Many CEOs have more of a looting mentality than a true concern for their citizenry. Many of the "captains of industry" are infatuated with the strategy of sucking every ounce of wealth out of as many people as possible.

What that translates into is that those of us, living under the tyranny of corporations, experience considerable upheaval in our lives. Corporations aren't interested in creating a harmonious environment. They're interested in making an environment that provokes consumers and which tends to be one of controlled chaotic bedlam, scarcity and rabid consumerism.

And no generation has been marketed to as heavily. We don't know the consequences of this yet, but we can figure that it is causing some new strains of neurosis and mental illness.

If we look at the marketing, the marketing is designed to evoke in us an artificial sense of desperation, an artificial sense of, "I need more. I'm empty. I lack. … Unless I have **THIS**."

Companies have studied how to get things to stick in our minds and which kinds of imagery are best suited to lodge suggestive material in our memory.

Children growing up are the most vulnerable and are being the most heavily marketed to. It is shaping their mindset for the rest of their lives.

Studies show that the way to get someone to remember something is to make them have an extremely intense emotional or physical sensation at the same time that they are exposed to whatever you want them to remember.

In a lab, scientists had people put their arms in ice and experience painful coldness at the same time that they were exposed to a sequence of numbers. Intense feelings heavily reinforced their memory of whatever was their focus in that moment. So it was, that people were much more able to remember strings of numbers, or random data, or a brand image, or a jingle when accompanied by an intense feeling or emotion. Intense feelings provide the energy to emblazon memories in our minds.

TV and media simulate experiences that alarm us on a primal level. Flashes of red, rapid cut editing, and unexpected shocks get our attention. If we look back 10,000 years ago, our ancestors had to be prepared for anything. When something flashed red through their field of vision, it often signaled a threat that had to be responded to instantly. Either predator or adversary would not wait for an appointment. We continue to be wired for responding to certain stimuli with an instant rush of adrenalin and the resultant vigor.

Certain stimuli are supposed to grab our attention immediately so that we can actively respond to them, but with TV simulating these primal alarms we're just supposed to sit there and passively accept such stimulation. The only socially appropriate response is to focus our attention on the TV, but this decision does all kinds of things to disturb our peace of mind.

Not exactly the tranquil hills of Switzerland with cows ringing their cowbells and just having to make the cheese everyday, now is it? It's a very different type of environment that we live in today.

Granted there are many benefits to our environment, in terms of offering us greater opportunities for wealth, health and extended life-spans, but we are paying the price in terms of quality of life experience. We are living in a time which is somewhat like the precursor to a neo Renaissance. We're being over stimulated by our technology and bombarded with stimuli that evoke primal, survival mechanisms. This may be prompting the activation of our DRD4 gene.

The great artists, inventors, trailblazers and thinkers of the Renaissance had the purpose of bringing balance back to their world. Before the Renaissance, society had been too chaotic and too troubled. The turmoil activated the genius in each of these great minds. When someone with the DRD4 genetic polymorphism experiences a deluge of life-threatening (or even just seemingly life-threatening) encounters, the DRD4 polymorphism activates and turns an ordinary craftsman into a brilliant warrior and innovator.

When this gene is activated it transforms complacency into restlessness. It unleashes a whole new reservoir of energy, vitality and genius. You find yourself noticing everything that's out of alignment – then feeling the irresistible need to fix it all! And if you won't let yourself start tackling the huge problems that you see, then you start going crazy from frustration. The DRD4 polymorphism is like an alarm bell waiting to go off – and when it goes off there's no stopping you. You become invincible.

Watch the montage from Rocky II and you'll see an awesome depiction of this principle in action. Literally, Rocky is given the green-light to honor his DRD4 activation when Adrian says, "Win!" and we watch him transform from an ordinary guy into a super hero. That's DRD4 in action. That's what this DRD4 DaVinci gene evolved to allow us to do.

When our ancestors were thrust into war, the ones who had the DRD4 polymorphism could transform on the spot from ordinary civilian to superhuman warrior. It's like watching the TV character David Banner's metamorphosis into the Incredible Hulk.

All these TV and movie sequences are based on an archetypal truth we all know on some level – that when a hero (a DaVinci type with the DRD4 polymorphism) is stirred, he doesn't just roll over like 90% of the general population would do – the hero transforms into a super hero. The DRD4 gene holds the key to that amazing metamorphosis.

During the pre-Renaissance period, people with the DRD4 polymorphism were stirred. Their genetic greatness was awakened and they turned into the superheroes that led the western world to a more elevated state of being. They led everyone from one expression of society which was chaotic, hurtful and upsetting, to something greater.

The DRD4 polymorphism could be a safety valve. When humanity gets too far out of hand, it awakens the superheroes, (the DaVincis), who, when stirred, bring balance back to the world.

Revolutions of Egalitarianism

The other thing about a Renaissance – or any kind of massive cultural change that someone like da Vinci would create – is that it's usually ushering in a new level of egalitarianism.

Da Vinci was very egalitarian. He didn't buy into hierarchies. Leonardo da Vinci did not buy into the superiority and inferiority implicit in hierarchies. Many thought this was probably due to his half-noble, half-common birth, but I believe this attitude towards human relations is part of the genetic DaVinci trait temperament.

DaVincis, in general, are suspicious of external authority. The DaVincis are rebels at heart. They tend to bow only to God – the Inner Authority. As far as outer relationships go, they only see equality with their fellow men, so they seek to manifest egalitarian relationships. That is not to say that DaVincis cannot be corrupted by power, for we are all still human. But for the most part DaVincis seek to discover the authority of Truth and worship only that, rather than bowing to a man-made throne.

"Anyone who conducts an argument by appealing
to authority is not using his intelligence;
he is just using his memory"

~ Leonardo da Vinci

Today, like throughout history, DaVincis are seen as a threat to authority. Many Normal types see DaVincis as threatening because they will not just become a cog in the wheel and stop "causing trouble" (i.e. causing change). Also the biggest multi-national corporations and pharmaceutical companies are now all intertwined and they have a huge stake in keeping the hierarchal system as it is.

DaVincis Abhor Hierarchy

Those with the activated DRD4 polymorphism tend to abhor hierarchy. They are contemptuous of inauthentic authority, because now the great leveling gene has taken over. Now they will answer to only one kind of authority and that's True Authority.

External, artificial authorities and hierarchies become the enemy. This is a time when the corporations are in power and they are the primary antagonists that are trying to suppress the expression of the DRD4 polymorphism. They have promoted the label of ADD/ADHD for those with the activated gene (especially the young ones) and they are medicating the life out of them.

You know it would definitely hurt their profits and diminish their workforce, if people weren't willing to work within their corporate hierarchal system of rewards and punishments – being good consumers and good employees. If the DaVincis are stirred and come alive, then their ivory towers collapse.

So our entire American school system is actually designed to destroy the DaVinci trait – or those who have it. It was originally developed by Germans right at the beginning of the Industrial Age in order to break people's spirits and shape them into good factory workers – good lifeless cogs in the wheel.

That's what corporations still want.

Corporate interests truly control our public schools because they shape our academic policy through their massive lobbying efforts. They decide where the money goes and how the money is spent and they even give grants to public schools if they host their Coke & Pepsi (caffeine) machines. Corporations want two things from our schools; good docile consumers, and good docile employees. That combination will ensure maximum profits and stability for our corporate empires.

George W. Bush began the No Child Left Behind Act, and the name is a mimetic nod to the "Left Behind" book phenomenon fueled by Christian fundamentalist movements. So while many of us heard "no child will be left behind in their schooling"– a significant group of voters hear that with this program "no child will be left behind by God when the Biblical End of Days arrives." Either way we can easily see this program is suspect and designed by corporations to further control our school systems.

Bush uses his language to make this corporate juggernaut sound like a good thing, "no child left behind", but really what it is is a way of controlling all the school systems centrally, through a series of budget defining standards. This further eliminates the ability of good teachers to offer vibrant and dynamic teaching. It also virtually eliminates the opportunity for anyone with the activated DRD4 DaVinci gene to benefit from that system, because really what's going to happen is that the rules are going to get stricter. The schools are going to become more and more afraid of not passing these quotas, therefore, the students that are DaVincis are going to be heavily medicated or kicked out of the schools, just because they're ruining the numbers.

There's nothing in the "no child left behind" act that says "innovation is valuable." Far from it, the act itself substitutes standardized test scores for alternate forms of innovative assessment. However, innovation and forward thinking is very valuable to many great teachers who recognize that creativity and innovation form the core of what our country is all about. However, it's not something that's easily recognized in a standardized test.

Schooling can be handled much more gracefully when you remove central control and trust in the ingenuity of teachers.

DaVincis Correct
What Corporations Corrupt

Corporations are inherently hierarchical. They are designed to control and shift power and wealth from the many to the few.

The powers that be are threatened by this potential new era of egalitarian beauty and the leveling of worldwide wealth. That's what the DaVinci led ONE Campaign is all about. Bono, a die-hard DaVinci type, started this powerful new organization of heavy-hitter DaVinci type movie stars, rock stars, religious leaders and politicians to level the playing field and make poverty history in our lifetime. I recommend that you find out more about it at One.org.

The United States – Founded by DaVincis

The other thing to recognize is that we, as Americans, do have a special place in the world, with regard to this genetic DRD4 polymorphism, because America is a place which people self-selected and moved to when they had the activated DRD4 polymorphism. It is probably no accident and very telling, if you'll recall the eagle in the chicken coop story, that the U.S. national bird is the bald eagle.

Other countries that have a population rich in DaVinci type pioneers are Australia, South Africa, and Canada.

The tendency to pursue adventure and adapt to new challenges was probably helpful when our ancestors first left Africa and started exploring the globe, Robert Moyzis says. He's a biochemist at the University of California, Irvine.

Research by Moyzis and his coworkers has shown that a certain form of a gene called DRD4 is more common in people descended from ancestors who traveled long distances to settle new areas than in descendants of those who stayed behind.

This gene form is also more common in kids who have been diagnosed with attention deficit hyperactivity disorder (ADHD) than in those who don't have the disorder. Kids who have ADHD find it hard to sit still and pay attention and tend to act without thinking.

~ Emily Sohn (ScienceNewsForKids.org)

The United States has a population that is a melting pot of heredity all leading back to one or another group of people who at one time said "I'm willing to risk everything just to find a better way – just to find a better place." Only people who have the DaVinci DRD4 polymorphism are apt to say that. And the people *without* the DaVinci trait are much more likely to just put up with what they've got.

The DRD4 polymorphism when activated causes one to want to adventure, explore, risk and pioneer new ventures.

What makes our country great is innovation. That's why we lead the world – at least economically and materially – because we've innovated so much. We've even innovated one of the most contagious cultures – look at McDonald's franchises, MTV, Rock music, blue jeans, baseball and the idea of democracy. All are ideas championed by American DaVincis and now these ideas have spread throughout the world, because our American culture rapidly evolves contagious ideas through our relentless innovation.

What makes culture compelling is its continual evolution to be most relevant to people's lives. North Americans are leaders in cultural evolution, material development and innovation because our population is full of Creative DaVinci types.

"The genius of you Americans is that you never make clear-cut stupid moves, only complicated stupid moves which make the rest of us wonder at the possibility that we might be missing something."

~ Gamal Abdel Nasser

What we're facing right now is a population so full of DaVinci types that we're experiencing a clash between the DaVincis and the bureaucrats (the Normal type). This is quite rare because usually DaVinci types are so scarce that it merely appears like there's one crazy genius up against the rest of the world. But now, because there is an insurgence of activated technology empowered DaVinci types, we're actually starting to feel a rift culturally between the DaVincis and the Normal types.

Saving Grace of America's Work Force

Maybe you haven't noticed, but India and China's knowledge-workforces are bigger and cheaper than those of the U.S. The same linear knowledge-worker job (like accounting, programming, x-ray examining, tech-support, engineering, etc.) done in North America for $50 an hour can be done just as well in India or China for $5 an hour. With telecommunications and remote collaborations tools making physical distance negligible, soon all competitive companies will outsource their most time intensive (least creative) knowledge work to India and China.

Where does that leave 50 million American knowledge-workers? Well to start with, jobless.

America's Inheritance

America is a melting pot of DaVinci types. At one time or another just about every country in the world has lost a percentage of its population to the American dream. And virtually all of those who would risk life and limb for such a far-out thing as "the American dream" would fit the DaVinci profile of risk-taking behavior – thus they would most likely carry the DaVinci gene.

America was colonized by DaVinci types - Adventurers, Explorers, Pioneers and the kind of risk takers that say "Hey this potato famine sucks, I'm outta here."

Because of this, North America has become the consolidating point for most of the DaVinci types of the world. North America has many more times DaVinci types in its population than any other area of the world.

There was a time when just surviving life was thrilling enough for our predominantly immigrant population – so generally, only the established descendants of the earlier immigrant generations were restless and educated enough to become business tycoons, innovators and artists. The business tycoons especially, eventually wanted to reinforce their accumulated power and wealth so they did what any self-serving victim of power corruption would do – they teamed up with other tyrants like themselves and developed systems and hierarchies designed to keep the rest of the population working for them. This is the dark side for the DaVinci.

A century later much of this industrial age oppression still exists while new avenues of opportunity have been carved by thousands of newly awakened DaVincis. Think Hollywood, Silicon Valley, and Wall Street.

Outsmarting Global Outsourcing

"Somebody has to do something and it's incredibly pathetic that it has to be us."

~ Jerry Garcia

Since its colonization, America has still led the world in innovation - a primary DaVinci quality. It is creativity and innovation that has made North America's economy great. It is creativity and innovation that will keep America great as millions of knowledge working jobs are moved overseas in the next 5 to 10 years.

Think about it: North America has a population of about 330 million. China has a population of 1.3 billion. And then add to that India's population of 1 billion people. That's 2 billion more people than in North America!

As India and China come online with their increasingly well educated workforces they'll be multiplying the global knowledge workforce by a factor of 10 or 20 in the coming years.

That means if you do a job that a well educated person from India or China could do just as easily non-locally, then you can expect to be asked to take a 90% pay cut in the coming years if you want to keep your job.

All you DaVincis out there, who've been playing the corporate employee card until now, it's time to Turn on, Tune in and Drop Out. Your linear corporate job is almost history. Your pension is being gambled with by corporate raiders. Bail out now and start doing something truly creative, innovative and entrepreneurial because the one thing the rest of the world can't compete with is the concentrated DaVinci gene pool that has been formed in America over four centuries of immigration.

DaVincis are the great innovators and leaders of culture, art and business. Maybe it's time to stop hiding in your cubicle and claim your place in this world as the trailblazer you were born to be. Now is the time for America to reinvent itself once again. Now is the time for America to claim its place as the world's think tank – the land of innovation, contagious culture and great art.

You are wasting your precious time if you are still working in an uncreative, uninventive, unadventurous career. That kind of career is evaporating in America.

You better be a creator, an innovator, a trailblazer, or a pioneer if you are a DaVinci. Don't wait until fate forces your hand, because fate can be harsh with those who ignore its early warnings.

Consider this your early warning.

Further Recommended Reading:

The Rise of the Creative Class: India, knowledge-worker outsourcing & you

A Whole New Mind: Moving from the Information Age to the Conceptual Age

The Flight of the Creative Class: The New Global Competition for Talent

Free Agent Nation: The Future of Working for Yourself

Schooling Revisited

"To sentence a man of true genius, to the drudgery
of a school is to put a racehorse on a treadmill."

~ Samuel Taylor Coleridge

The following is an edited transcript of the 2005 Commencement address made at Stanford by an exemplary DaVinci type, Steve Jobs, CEO of Apple Computer and of Pixar Animation Studios:

Thank you. I'm honored to be with you today for your commencement from one of the finest universities in the world. Truth be told, I never graduated from college and this is the closest I've ever gotten to a college graduation.

I dropped out of Reed College after the first six months but then stayed around as a drop-in for another 18 months or so before I really quit.

I naively chose a college that was almost as expensive as Stanford, and all of my working-class parents' savings were being spent on my college tuition.

After six months, I couldn't see the value in it. I had no idea what I wanted to do with my life, and no idea of how college was going to help me figure it out. And here I was, spending all the money my parents had saved their entire life. So I decided to drop out and trust that it would all work out OK. It was pretty scary at the time, but looking back, it was one of the best decisions I ever made. The minute I dropped out, I could stop taking the required classes that didn't interest me and begin dropping in on the ones that looked far more interesting.

"Just as eating contrary to the inclination is injurious to the health, so study without desire sports the memory, and it retains nothing that it takes in."

~ Leonardo da Vinci

It wasn't all romantic. I didn't have a dorm room so I slept on the floor in friends' rooms. I returned Coke bottles for the 5-cent deposits to buy food with, and I would walk the 7 miles across town every Sunday night to get one good meal a week at the Hare Krishna temple.

I loved it. And much of what I stumbled into by following my curiosity and intuition turned out to be priceless later on. Let me give you one example.

Reed College at that time offered perhaps the best calligraphy instruction in the country. Throughout the campus every poster, every label on every drawer was beautifully hand-calligraphed.

Because I had dropped out and didn't have to take the normal classes, I decided to take a calligraphy class to learn how to do this. I learned about serif and sans serif typefaces, about varying the amount of space between different letter combinations, about what makes great typography great. It was beautiful, historical, artistically subtle in a way that science can't capture, and I found it fascinating.

None of this had even a hope of any practical application in my life. But 10 years later when we were designing the first Macintosh computer, it all came back to me, and we designed it all into the Mac.

It was the first computer with beautiful typography. If I had never dropped in on that single course in college, the Mac would have never had multiple typefaces or proportionally spaced fonts, and since Windows just copied the Mac, it's likely that no personal computer would have them. If I had never dropped out, I would have never dropped in on that calligraphy class and personal computers might not have the wonderful typography that they do.

Of course it was impossible to connect the dots looking forward when I was in college, but it was very, very clear looking backward 10 years later.

Again, you can't connect the dots looking forward. You can only connect them looking backward, so you have to trust that the dots will somehow connect in your future. You have to trust in something your gut, destiny, life, karma, whatever because believing that the dots will connect down the road will give you the confidence to follow your heart, even when it leads you off the well-worn path, and that will make all the difference.

I was lucky I found what I loved to do early in life. Woz [Steve Wozniak] and I started Apple in my parents' garage when I was 20. We worked hard, and in 10 years, Apple had grown from just the two of us in a garage into a $2 billion company with over 4,000 employees. We'd just released our finest creation, the Macintosh, a year earlier, and I'd just turned 30, and then I got fired.

I was still in love. And so I decided to start over.

I didn't see it then, but it turned out that getting fired from Apple was the best thing that could have ever happened to me. The heaviness of being successful was replaced by the lightness of being a beginner again, less sure about everything. It freed me to enter one of the most creative periods in my life.

During the next five years I started a company named NeXT, another company named Pixar and fell in love with an amazing woman who would become my wife. Pixar went on to create the world's first computer-animated feature film, Toy Story, and is now the most successful animation studio in the world.

In a remarkable turn of events, Apple bought NeXT and I returned to Apple.

And the technology we developed at NeXT is at the heart of Apple's current renaissance, and Laurene and I have a wonderful family together.

I'm pretty sure none of this would have happened if I hadn't been fired from Apple.

Don't lose faith. I'm convinced that the only thing that kept me going was that I loved what I did. You've got to find what you love, and that is as true for work as it is for your lovers. Your work is going to fill a large part of your life, and the only way to be truly satisfied is to do what you believe is great work, and the only way to do great work is to love what you do.

If you haven't found it yet, keep looking and don't settle. As with all matters of the heart, you'll know when you find it, and like any great relationship it just gets better and better as the years roll on. So keep looking. Don't settle.

Remembering that I'll be dead soon is the most important tool I've ever encountered to help me make the big choices in life. Because almost everything all external expectations, all pride, all fear of embarrassment or failure; these things just fall away in the face of death, leaving only what is truly important.

Remembering that you are going to die is the best way I know to avoid the trap of thinking you have something to lose. You are already naked.

There is no reason not to follow your heart.

Death is very likely the single best invention of life. It's life's change agent; it clears out the old to make way for the new. Right now, the new is you. But someday not too long from now, you will gradually become the old and be cleared away. Sorry to be so dramatic, but it's quite true.

Your time is limited, so don't waste it living someone else's life. Don't be trapped by dogma, which is living with the results of other people's thinking. Don't let the noise of others' opinions drown out your own inner voice, and most important, have the courage to follow your heart and intuition. They somehow already know what you truly want to become.

Everything else is secondary.

Stay Hungry. Stay Foolish.

Thank you all very much."

~ Steve Jobs

*"I know that I am not a man of letters
[i.e. not formally educated]
Experience is my one true mistress
and I will sight her in all cases.*

*Only through Experimentation
can we truly know ANYTHING."*

~ Leonardo da Vinci

The Qualities of a DaVinci

The following qualities seem to fit the temperament of most DaVincis. See if you recognize them:

- ✓ Restless
- ✓ Impulsive
- ✓ Irrepressible (or not having much repression.)
- ✓ Energetic
- ✓ Non-conformist
- ✓ Rebellious
- ✓ Energetic
- ✓ Charismatic
- ✓ Thrill-seeking
- ✓ Ambitious
- ✓ Inquisitive
- ✓ Fearless
- ✓ Lateral-thinker
- ✓ Creative
- ✓ Holistically minded
- ✓ Looks at the "Big Picture"
- ✓ Hyper-focused & Driven at times
- ✓ "Lazy" at other times
- ✓ Runs hot and Cold
- ✓ Sexually driven
- ✓ Hot tempered

Who else is a DaVinci?

*"We all have the 'slightly crazy' gene that is
continually going to pop up throughout our lives,
no matter how under control we think we are."*

~ Sylvester Stallone

The following is a short list of the names of well known people who had many, (if not all), of the above "Qualities of a DaVinci". It is most likely that they too had the activated DaVinci gene (the DRD4 polymorphism).

This list could be much more extensive, because DaVinci types make up to 5% of the world population over the course of history. However the list is merely intended to show how the traits of the DRD4 polymorphism have a high correlation with one's ability to attain incredible success and genius. These people are rebels, risk takers, out-of-the-box thinkers, and charismatic, impulsive and often sexually promiscuous – all traits of the DaVinci temperament.

- Napoleon
- Thomas Jefferson
- Bill Clinton
- Benjamin Franklin
- Thomas Edison
- Winston Churchill
- Bono (lead singer for U2)
- John F. Kennedy (In fact most of the Kennedys are, since this is genetic.)
- Abraham Lincoln
- Oprah Winfrey

- Billy Idol
- Richard Branson (founder of Virgin)
- Steve Jobs (founder of Apple & Pixar)
- Conan O'Brien (late night comedian)
- Joe DiMaggio
- Vincent van Gogh
- Sylvester Stallone
- Michael Jordan
- Bode Miller (World Champion Skier)
- Larry Ellison (founder of Oracle)
- Timothy Leary
- Elvis Presley
- Steven Spielberg
- Donald Trump
- Dave Neeleman (CEO jetBlue)
- Dean Kamen (prolific inventor of Segway)
- George Lucas
- Salvador Dali
- Marianne Williamson (best-selling author)
- Otto Rank (brilliant psychologist)
- Carl Jung
- Robin Williams

Add to this list of DaVincis most great athletes, police officers, firemen, EMTs, paramedics, emergency room nurses, jet pilots (especially fighter pilots), warriors, generals, inventors, salespeople, crisis management consultants, stock traders, artists, rock stars, mystics, pioneers, explorers, entrepreneurs, mavericks and revolutionaries; then you'll get a pretty good idea about the group we're talking about here.

Want to see a huge list of famous DaVincis?

Go to: **www.DaVinciMethod.com/famous**

Are you still a DaVinci?

"I don't want to be a genius - I have enough problems just trying to be a man"

~ Albert Camus

If you're still reading this, chances are something has piqued your interest and you resonate with the idea of the DaVinci trait, with the DaVinci mindset and you probably are a DaVinci yourself.

Now that does not mean that you're a great inventor or entrepreneur or artist or leader … yet.

But you can be.

You know it's rare that one is able to cultivate their DaVinci trait well enough to experience the benefits of it but The DaVinci Method is designed to help you get there, to help you become a great creator, one who is both successful and rewarded for your creations and also greatly helpful to the world around you, one who is going to usher in the new age of innovation, and a greater time of peace and harmony in our world.

What the world needs now is genuine benevolent leadership. You as DaVinci have a great potential to lead. The time to begin your leadership is now.

So let's get started …

Welcome to
The DaVinci Method.

*"You can have no dominion greater or less than
that over yourself."*

~ Leonardo da Vinci

The DaVinci Method is a therapy program specifically designed for the 10% of our population who carry the same genetic predisposition for genius that Leonardo da Vinci had.

This is a way to access that supernatural force that led Leonardo DaVinci to make amazing discoveries, harness superhuman physical strength, and create works of sublime beauty. This is a path to the universal and limitless power inside of you, the chosen ones with the DaVinci trait.

The chosen ones are Self chosen, because the DaVinci trait is actually a Self activated gene, meaning the expression of the DRD4 7 allele repeat DaVinci gene is literally ignored or activated through your own experience.

This is a path to surrendering to constructively realizing the power your soul has chosen for you. This is a path to limitlessness. This is a path to discovering your truest potential.

*"Your job as an artist, inventor, entrepreneur, or
leader is to transcend limits. You find the burden,
the dead area of your life, and resurrect it.*

*Your resurrection is then shared with the world
and inspires others to do the same."*

~ Garret LoPorto

People of the DaVinci Type either tend to be phenomenally successful at what they do – like Richard Branson, John F Kennedy, Thomas Edison, David Neeleman (CEO of JetBlue), Bono (Singer for U2) – or they crash and burn, it all depends on where they're coming from.

The DaVinci Method teaches you about the two places that you can be coming from – the "artist" or the "neurotic."

The artist is creative and productive. His abundant creative energies move from his inner world to his outer world shaping the outer world in his own image. His awareness of messages from his powerful unconscious offers him brilliance in the face of adversity, depth in the face of mediocrity, and power in solving impossible problems. Through practice he has become confident that he can effectively communicate the unspeakable mysteries of his inner world into an outer form that his community can understand. He is irrepressible, prolific and confident. His inner guidance, powerful impulses, honesty and courage allows him to discover and master the truth in himself and his world and thus become great.

The neurotic has access to all of the power of the artist, but is afraid to use it. He has turned his creative energies against himself in an effort to control his outer appearance. He doesn't express himself. Instead he represses himself with white knuckle effort. He second-guesses his instincts; plus his awareness of messages from his powerful unconscious only confuses him more. He doesn't trust himself or the world, so he hides. He hides what he knows and tries to consciously control what he expresses outwardly instead of being confident and trusting of his inner guidance, wisdom and spontaneous impulses. He becomes mechanical and controlling in the face of the uncertainty of both his inner and outer worlds. Instead of surfing the powerful tides of the great unconscious, (like the confident artist does), he fights them like a scared child. In order to avoid the thrilling freefall he was born to surrender to, he hesitates, procrastinates, lies to himself, and fakes being much less than he is.

*"Christ said that what he does, you, too, shall do,
and even greater"*

~ John 14:12

The DaVinci Method helps you overcome the neurotic tendencies you may still wrestle with and helps you finally become the "Artist" of your own destiny.

DaVincis:
Artistic or Neurotic?

The DaVinci types

A DaVinci type has a particularly strong tendency towards the glorification of his own will. Unlike the average citizen, he feels compelled to remake reality in his own image. He is conscious of his immutable unconscious desire for immortality, which he can only achieve by identifying himself with the collective unconscious, or the will of God.

Great art can be understood as a joining of the material and the spiritual, the specific and the universal, the individual and humanity.

This joining doesn't come easily. It begins with the *will*, Otto Rank's word for the power of choice. Will is the prize your consciousness awards to your ego or to your soul, depending on which has your attention for the moment. So, each moment, you will either experience *will* in the form of your ego's will or *Will* in the form of your soul's will depending on whether you choose to be in ego awareness or soul awareness at that moment.

We are all born with a will to be ourselves, to be free of domination. In early childhood, we exercise our will in our efforts to do things independently of our parents. Later, we fight the domination of other authorities, including the inner authority of our soul and the inner tyranny of our bodily and ego drives.

How our struggle for independence goes determines the type of person we become. Rank describes three basic types:

Firstly, and most common, is the **Normal type**. These people learn to adapt their "will" to what they have been forced to do. They obey external authority, their society's moral code, and, as best as they can, their sexual impulses. This is a passive, duty-bound citizen that Rank says is the average person.

Second, there is the **neurotic type – or anxious type**. These people have a much stronger will than the average person, but it is totally engaged in the fight against external and internal domination. They even fight the expression of their own will, so there is no will left over to actually do anything with the freedom they have won. Instead, they worry and feel guilty about being so "willful." They are, however, at a higher level of moral development than the adapted type.

Third, there is **the Creative type – or productive type**, which Otto Rank refers to as the Artist, the genius, the creative type, and the 'total human'. Instead of fighting themselves, Artistic types accept and affirm themselves, and create an ideal, which functions as a positive focus for will. The artist creates himself, and then creates his world in his image. [4]

"There are three classes of people: Those who see.
Those who see when they are shown.
Those who do not see."

~ Leonardo da Vinci

According to Leonardo da Vinci's quote it can be readily seen that of the three classes of people, the first class "those who see" are the artistic type, the second class "those who see when they are shown" are the neurotic type and finally "those who do not see" constitute the Normal type.

The Artist & the Neurotic

Artist

n. a person whose work shows exceptional creative ability, sensitivity and imagination.

neu·rot·ic

adj. Overanxious

n. a person prone to excessive anxiety and emotional upset.

The Artist and the neurotic both live from the subconscious and unconscious depths of themselves and society. The Artist does this productively, communicating his experiences of the deep unsettling truths – discovered in his unconscious – in positive ways to his community. The Artist is a leader because he makes it desirable to follow his way. On the other hand, the neurotic fails to effectively communicate his experiences of the deep unsettling symbols and contradictions he encounters in his unconscious. So in shame, he turns inward and away from his fellow man, thus he forsakes his opportunity to lead and to heal.

Both Artist and neurotic are like canaries in the mine shaft. They will be the first to experience coming shifts in the cultural environment that are afoot and the Artist may shape or even appear to be the bringer of that change. Since great art springs from the unconscious, it offers us a portrayal of our collective experience. This may yet only be present to the DaVincis who, by virtue of their sensitivity to the collective unconscious grumblings and stirs of the soul, live on the frontier of their culture's consciousness.

Since both the Artist and the neurotic live out of the unconscious mind, they are intimately and consciously tied into what most people in society are living out unconsciously. The neurotic is exposed to the same unconscious stirrings as the Artist, but the neurotic fails to give these stirrings he senses a productive outlet. His energy backs up in him like a hose with a knot in it. He puts himself under great pressure because he can neither deny the stirrings of his unconscious mind, nor does he muster the courage to release these insights into his world through creative acts. He is left stuck, and frustrated, and bursting at the seams with the bile of unexpressed genius.

Otto Rank said the neurotic is the "artiste manqué," (the frustrated artist), because he refuses to transmute his impulses into art.

Otto Rank's Will Therapy

Otto Rank was the most creative of Freud's protégés. Because his foremost therapy "Will Therapy" was designed exclusively for DaVinci types, his therapy really only applies to a mere 10% of the general population. This has led to a relative forgetting of his contribution for lack of awareness of to whom it applies, since it only works for 1 out of 10 people.

Nowadays we have become more aware of a diagnosable disorder called ADD/ADHD – the dark side of the DaVinci type (or 'total human' as Rank would say) – we can now find a suitable place for Rank's powerful Will Therapy to operate. Thus we can bring healing to the ADD/ADHD "neurotic" type and help them become Rank's "artist" or "productive" type.

If you would like to learn more directly about Otto Rank's theory, his most important works are **Art and Artist**, **Truth and Reality**, and **Will Therapy**. Furthermore, a major aspect of the therapy in The DaVinci Method is firmly based on Rank's Will Therapy.

Proper Art

In his early autobiographical novel *A Portrait of the Artist As a Young Man*, James Joyce's *alter ego*, Stephen Dedalus, draws on Aristotle in a discussion of aesthetics, where he distinguishes between improper and proper art. The former is *kinetic*, meaning its purpose is to excite and elicit emotional movement in the observer, listener, or reader, as in pornographic or didactic art. The focus of the creator here is external, for it is on the audience's response.

Proper art, Stephen continues, is *static*, insofar as it is interested only in the art itself -- the internal -- not its elicited or desired reaction. We may extend this understanding not only to artists as creators, but as performers. Whereas creators can be faithful to their inspiring Muse and not to the art's effect on others, performers likewise can be faithful to the inspiration's source, and not to their special ability to arouse emotion in their audiences.

A discerning public can tell the difference between *proper* and *improper* artists and performers; those who remain true to the genius of the inspiration as opposed to those who care only for the external gratifications -- in Freud's famous words regarding the artist: the pursuit of honor, power, and love.

~ Kenneth Wapnick, Ph. D.

Art Forbears Science

Art forbears science. Eros attracts Logos and together they conceive genius. Before scientific discoveries are made, muses whisper the secrets through an artist's work. Before a great idea is hatched, it has already been danced. Life is music so the only way to understand it is to feel it first.

Let us allow gifted perception to create a vision for what is to come. Let us dance the dance scientists will someday validate with rigorous reason.

*"Talking about music is like
dancing about architecture."*

~ Steve Martin

As part of embracing and nurturing our artistic productive nature, we begin with the understanding that we will *never* understand. You don't find your rhythm and "groove" on a dance floor by analyzing the tempo and measure of the music and following some prescription for how one should move to that frequency. You just feel it. You let that feeling connect the music with something deep inside you, your body becomes part of the union between the music and your soul and you express that union from inside out.

Said another way, some things are so profoundly beyond our current mental frameworks that the only way to express them is through something abstract enough to conjure a feeling and maybe a glimpse of what is to come. Here is how Joseph Campbell relates this nuance of the indescribable:

Speaking to a Japanese Shinto priest, a social philosopher from New York remarked:

*"I've been now to a good many ceremonies and
have seen quite a few of your shrines. But I don't
get your ideology. I don't get your theology."*

The priest paused as though in deep thought and then slowly shook his head.

"I think we don't have ideology.

We don't have theology.

We dance."

~ Joseph Campbell – The Power of Myth

The same is true for great leadership and art. To be a great leader or artist you don't merely regurgitate what you're seeing in the outer world processed through your sophisticated set of "art" or "leadership" principles. Instead you allow your soul to genuinely encounter what you are experiencing and then you must have the courage to honestly express the product of that encounter – the impetus that the encounter has conceived in you.

Take for example, a great moment in football. On November 20th, 1982 the California Bears encountered a situation they never expected, they were down by one point with only seconds left on the clock. There is no "plan" or "principle" that can help you win in this kind of situation. The only thing that can possibly prevail is the kind of genius we can only call miraculous.

In this particular encounter a few courageous football players pulled off one of the all time greatest moments in football. With an unbelievable 57-yard kickoff return that included five laterals, Kevin Moen runs through Stanford band members who had prematurely come onto the field. His touchdown stands and California wins 25-20.

You can see and hear this extraordinary moment of cooperative brilliance by going to this URL:

www.DaVinciMethod.com/greatmoments

And here's Kevin Moen's account of what happened:

Announcer: "Stanford hits it with 4 seconds to go! And takes the lead 20-19! Only a miracle could save the Bears as Stanford piles out on the field."

Kevin Moen (California running-back):

It's hard to describe the feeling on the Cal sideline at that moment. Quiet desperation hit the team. We were missing a player as we lined up for the kickoff, so I moved over to cover the vacant area. The kick bounced to me. After making the catch, I remembered "grab-ass," one of Coach Kapp's training games. It had no rules, just one bunch of guys trying to keep the ball away from another bunch of guys.

My first thought after receiving the kick was simply to run the ball all the way back for a touchdown, but when I noticed a group of Stanford players running at me I decided to reevaluate that plan. I glanced left and saw Richard Rogers waving from near the sideline. He seemed to expect me to throw him the ball, so I did. Apparently Richard also had plans to run for a touchdown but, stalled by the Stanford defense, he pitched the ball to freshman Dwight Garner. Garner seemed to want to be a hero, too, and run over five Stanford guys on his way to the end zone, but reality set in just before Dwight's knee hit the ground.

Things were really getting interesting now. Suddenly Richard had the ball again. He took off down the field, and I trailed behind in perfect tailback-option position. He ran at a Stanford player, made a good read, and tossed a flawless pitch back towards me. Mariet Ford came flying up, snagged the pitch instead, and took off.

By now I was kind of curious to see how things would unfold, so I followed Mariet upfield. Before long, a couple of Stanford players got close, and Mariet decided to do a diving, no-look, over-the-shoulder toss back to me. I still don't understand how he knew I was there. As the ball floated down into my hands, things were getting really strange. Stanford band members were all over the field! By this point I was thinking that it really was time to get into the end zone. Wes Howell blocked the last defender in my way, and I plowed on through the band. I could see the end zone through a cloud of red, and once I crossed the line I started my celebration.

Memorial Stadium went crazy. When the cannon went off, it was pandemonium. Cal fans poured onto the field. Did I mention the eerie silence and stunned disbelief emanating from the Stanford section? Nobody knew exactly what had happened; in the haze of the Play even I was not sure what had taken place. But everyone was running around hugging each other. It was the start of a celebration that would last a lifetime.

It's hard to believe that, 20 years later, the buzz of the Play is still so strong. Whenever I see the Play--or better yet, hear Joe Starkey call it--a smile comes to my face. Everyone seems to have something to say about that Big Game. All I can say is: Thank God I didn't fumble."

The Artist is a Hero of Our Age

The Artist is a productive DaVinci type living out his own hero's journey to be experienced vicariously by the rest of the populace. His art is the elixir won on his journey. He then shares that elixir with his community and if that elixir is relevant then he is rewarded with fame.

Therefore an artist must continue to make new inner journeys in order to stay relevant. He must become relevant anew with each and every new cultural movement.

Alpha & Theta DaVinci Sub-types

There are two sub-types of DaVincis – the Alpha DaVinci type, which is assertive, scientific, realistic, grounded, practical, externally aware, pragmatic, and has good gut instincts. You might say Alpha DaVinci types are "realists" and have their feet firmly planted on the ground.

Alpha types make great entrepreneurs, athletes, rescue workers, fighter jet pilots, trial lawyers, salespeople, scientists, and political leaders.

Then there is the Theta DaVinci type which is receptive, intuitive, artistic, dreamy, inspired and visionary. You might say Theta DaVinci types are inspired "idealists" and "dreamers" with their heads in the clouds.

Theta types make great artists, musicians, filmmakers, healers, writers, inventors, visionaries, mystics and spiritual leaders.

Which one are you?

If you are an Alpha DaVinci type who likes hard-nosed science and externally verifiable data, the next few sections will probably please you the most.

However, if you are more of a Theta DaVinci type then you may find the next section on brainwaves to be a bit science heavy and not inspirational enough for your tastes. You'll probably enjoy the later sections of this book most, where we begin to explore the more elevated, inspiring aspects of your DaVinci nature.

Unique Brainwaves of the DaVinci

The Four Brainwave States

There are four primary brain wave ranges, which are Beta, Alpha, Theta and Delta. These make up the EEG, which is short for electroencephalogram. Brainwaves are tiny oscillating electrical voltages in the brain; each wave is just a few millionths of a volt.

Your brain wave activity incorporates Beta, Alpha, Theta, and Delta frequencies at varying levels over the course of a day as your brain modulates them to match your activities. You could think of changing brainwave levels like a stereo equalizer where you can turn up or down various frequency ranges – or you could think of changing brainwave levels like an orchestra where each instrument represents a unique frequency that can play high or low, fast or slow, indulge a solo, or play in or out of time and harmony with the other instruments.

Beta

Alertness
Concentration
Cognition

Beta waves range between 13-40 HZ. The Beta state correlates with peak concentration, heightened alertness, eye-hand coordination and visual acuity.

When your brain is high in Beta activity, you are wide-awake, alert. Your mind is sharp, focused. You are primed to do work that requires your full externally focused attention. In the Beta state, neurons fire, in rapid succession (sometimes frenetically), helping you achieve rapid reactive performance. Habitual & reactive ideas and solutions to problems are available quickly to your brain – like a computer rapidly running its programming.

Increased Beta brainwaves give you mental alertness and higher levels of external concentration which can help you prepare to take an exam, exercise, give a rote presentation, and analyze and organize information quickly and efficiently. Abundant activity in this brainwave range also increases your stress levels.

EEG Beta training is one of the frequencies that biofeedback therapists use to treat Attention Deficit Disorder. This therapy can help a DaVinci "wake up" to the outer world more and think linearly and methodically like the Normal type.

Alpha

The Zone
Calmness
Visualization
Creativity
Flow

When you are truly calm and awake, when you are in "the zone" described by high-performance athletes, your brain activity is resonating in harmonic Alpha wave patterns. Your awareness expands and flows with creative energy. Fears and anxieties that may have existed in a predominantly Beta wave driven state will dissolve into courageous clarity in Alpha state.

An abundance of Alpha waves shifts your waking experience to a sublime, liberating sense of peace and well-being.

Alpha-centered brainwave states help you tap your creativity, solve difficult problems, discover new approaches and practice creative visualization. Alpha offers you mental clarity along with the tranquility essential to your health, wealth and well-being.

Alpha waves range between 7-12 HZ. This is a waking place of inner stillness, but not deep meditation.

In the lower range of Alpha (around 7-8 Hz) you can access the wealth of creativity that lies just below your conscious awareness - it is the gateway, the entry point that leads into deeper states of consciousness. This gateway is between 7.5 – 7.8 Hz which is the resonant frequency of the earth's electromagnetic field. This frequency is known as the Schuman Resonance and seems to correlate with the optimal vibration of life on this planet. When your brain resonates at this point you have placed your mind in true harmony with life; you may feel your whole being buzz and tingle with electricity; and you are anchored in a spiritual transcendence known as the Way, the Truth and the Life. This is your sweet spot. This is ideally where you want to center the weight of your consciousness.

Theta

Deep Meditation
Intuition
Memory
Mysticism
Hallucinating, Dreaming

Theta waves range between 4-8 HZ. Theta is the realm of the smoldering subconscious, and the semi–conscious gateway to the mysterious unconscious. It is the twilight state which we experience fleetingly as we fall into dreaming, while we are dreaming and right as we awaken from a dream. It is full of vivid imagery, rejected psychic material, flashes of insight, and the inspiration of genius.

Theta has also been identified as the area of long-term learning and memory. Theta meditation enhances learning capacity, reduces stress and awakens intuition and other extrasensory perception skills.

A deep meditation in Theta brings forward heightened receptivity, flashes of dreamlike imagery, inspiration, and your long-forgotten memories and a sensation of "floating." While your consciousness is centered in Theta, you may feel your mind expand beyond the boundaries of your body.

Theta sits on the threshold of your subconscious/ unconscious mind. Brainwaves in this range engage the places where you hold memories and underlying emotions. We can store secrets, which we feel unprepared to fix, in this subconscious/unconscious realm. These secrets may haunt us in our dreams but they will most likely be masked by ornate symbolism, allowing us to ignore them until we are ready.

Finally, Theta is an ideal state for super-learning, re-programming your subconscious mind, dream recollection, and hypnosis.

Drug and alcohol addicts may feel a scarcity of Theta, which perpetuates their cravings for artificial means to slow their overall brainwave state. More Theta rich brainwave states can be achieved with biofeedback and audio brainwave entrainment, which has been shown to reduce alcohol and drug dependency.

"Frontal Midline Theta (Fmθ) is a specific EEG frequency seen in those subjects actively engaged in cognitive activity, such as solving math problems and playing Tetris®, a Nintendo® game. The peak frequency is between 6.2 and 6.7 Hz. ...

Fm Theta is associated clinically with the ability to sustain attention over a time, an extroverted personality, low anxiety and low neuroticism. ... Of importance, the administration of diazepam (Valium®) and the ingestion of alcohol increases Fm Theta. ...

In a study of those with marked extroversion, Fm Theta was found, along with lowered platelet MAO activity [Low platelet MAO activity is associated with 'type 2 alcoholism.' MAO activity is also affected by cigarette smoking]"

~ Journal of Neurotherapy:
Theta: Don't Tread on Me[5]

Delta

Healing
Deep Sleep
Detached Awareness

Delta waves range between 0-4 HZ. These are long, slow, rising and falling waveforms. Delta is the slowest of all four brain wave frequency ranges. It is associated with deep sleep, and certain frequencies in the Delta range trigger the release of Human Growth Hormone, which can be beneficial for healing and regeneration. This is why deep, Delta rich, restorative sleep is essential to the physical healing process.

Delta is the brain wave signal of the unconscious. If you want to access your unconscious activity you may need to meditate so deeply that you are still conscious in an increased Delta state.

Why is Alpha Special?

Alpha waves oscillate at about 10 times per second, with a range between 7-13 cycles per second.

Alpha is not the highest or the lowest band of brainwave frequencies. Beta is the highest frequency band and Delta is the lowest. The reason the mid-range brain waves are called "Alpha" is because it was the first range to be discovered (around 1908, by an Austrian Psychiatrist named Hans Berger). Alpha is the first letter of the Greek alphabet.

In deep sleep there is little to no Alpha, and if someone is highly aroused in fear or anger, there is virtually no Alpha – it is all Beta. Delta is evident in the deepest stages of sleep (Stages 3 and 4). Theta is seen in REM, dreaming sleep and drowsiness (sleep stages 1 and 2). Alpha is most available in wakefulness where there is a relaxed and effortless alertness. Beta is most prominent in high alertness, highly stressful situations, and when there is difficult mental concentration and focus.

Most Normal types (and now many DaVinci types jacked up on caffeine or Ritalin) experience very little in the realm of Theta and Alpha brainwaves. The consequences of this are a constricted state of low but consistent and steady productivity and very little room for spontaneous inspiration or activity.

These people often wake up out of a deep sleep (predominantly Delta waves) with an alarm. Then they immediately move their brainwave state into the hyper-vigilant externalized and predominantly Beta brain state – they may have to drink coffee or soda, take diet pills or take Ritalin to force themselves into a Beta intensive wakefulness. The caffeine or methylphenidate (Ritalin) suppresses Theta and Alpha, while only promoting Beta.[6]

All day working under stress, pressure, and time urgency causes the brain to stay pinned in Beta, until at night, people fall exhausted into deep sleep (Delta), having spent little to no time calmly unwinding, relaxing, and allowing their mind to meditate or drift (which would give an opportunity for Alpha and Theta to increase). Thus many people suddenly and forcefully shift their brains back and forth from Delta to Beta, and then back to Delta again without ever spending time in the realm of the soul Alpha and Theta.

People who have increased Alpha brain waves have less anxiety and, correspondingly, stronger immune systems. True creativity also requires increased Alpha and Theta brain activity. Scientists have shown that highly creative people – DaVinci types – have different brainwave patterns from normal and non-creative people (Normal types). In order to have creative inspiration, your brain needs to be able to generate a surge of Alpha and Theta activity. The brains of DaVinci types – especially the Artistic DaVinci type – can generate these Alpha/Theta surges, and do so when they are faced with difficult problems to solve. Normal type people do not produce Alpha increases when they are faced with problems, and so they cannot come up with creative ideas and solutions. Any time you have an insight or an inspiration, you know your brain just produced more Alpha and Theta waves than usual.

The Zone

Peak performance is another activity for which Alpha is necessary. Sports scientists have shown that increases of Alpha brainwaves precede peak performance. One key difference between a novice and an elite athlete is in their brain waves. Just before his best free throws, an elite basketball player will produce a surge of Alpha waves in their brain. Just before their best strokes, elite golfers will produce surges of Alpha waves in their brain. Just before their best shots, elite marksmen and archers will produce a surge of Alpha waves in their left brains. Novice and intermediate athletes do not show this increased Alpha pattern.

One study showed that as novice archers trained over many weeks, their improved performance corresponded to gradually increasing surges of Alpha waves just before their best shots. Increased Alpha brainwaves are essential for entering "the zone" of peak performance. [7]

DaVincis are born gifted with creativity and innate access to "the zone" for reaching astounding athletic prowess. Have you managed to keep that ability? If not, take heart. You can get back to it. Keep reading.

Getting in the Zone–Getting into Alpha

Energy Surge + Alpha/Theta = Genius

The amount of energy fueling your brain at the moment determines how many bands of brainwaves you can sustain in that moment. When your brain is low in energy only a few frequency bands of brainwaves will be detectable. However, when you have harnessed your creative energies – your soul power – and elevated that energy to the level of the mind, you set your mind ablaze and you are receptive to the levels of genius while conscious enough to communicate your moment of genius into the world. This is the genius of the great artists.

Creative/sexual energy is what must be properly channeled to accomplish this. It is a genuine encounter with beauty that evokes inspiration – a surge of creative energy or will – in you. Beauty can be found anywhere, even in the most difficult situations. It is the willingness to behold the beauty in each moment that rewards one with a positive surge of inspiration, energy and direction.

DaVincis being of minimal repression are more powerfully moved by every encounter, especially because the impulse-to-join, which each encounter evokes, wells up much closer to the surface of consciousness and thus manifests more prominently in consciousness. These impulses can literally eclipse the ego-framework and overwhelm a DaVinci's conscious mind.

That is why these impulses can not effectively be controlled consciously. The conscious mind is too limited to direct this surge of psychic energy fruitfully. It's like trying to hit a baseball or a golf ball well, while thinking consciously about the way every part of your body is moving. It simply won't work. There's not enough room in the conscious mind to house all that information. It must be guided by a higher intelligence.

The Alpha Male *Stays* in Alpha

An interesting thing about language is that it is symbolic and thus offers many clues through puns and identical words used to describe seemingly disconnected things.

One nice example of this is the "Alpha male." Alpha male traditionally describes the dominant male of a group. But what makes that male superior to the other males? Often it is merely strength and stature, but with human beings strength is not merely physical, it is also mental, emotional and spiritual. I reckon the true Alpha male of any human group is the male who can sustain himself the most consistently in his "zone" of power (the Alpha brainwave state) without being intimidated into the less powerful Beta (panic) brainwave state.

Sex Drugs & Rock & Roll

Sex

Making love is a creative encounter and release that helps bring a DaVinci present. DaVincis tend to love sex because it puts them into an Alpha rich brainwave state, sometimes even Theta (you know, if it's *that* good). Good sex, mixed with love, creates a momentary union of two souls. Alpha (Will) reaching into Theta (Love) is the bridge over which the soul speaks.

Sexuality & Will

Sexual energy and the energy of will power are much the same thing. Willfulness and horniness are coming from basically the same place. Artistic passion and romantic passion are expressing a very similar kind of bliss.

In order to develop your will, which is the fire that propels you to success, you must cultivate and channel your sexual energy.

For some DaVincis who experience an abundance of motivation, drive and fire, and have learned to channel this fire into the accomplishment of their aims, this is a non-issue.

While for other DaVinci types who experience plenty of drive, but only for indulgences like sex, food, and drugs or alcohol this will be a matter of discipline.

And finally, for DaVincis caught in the downward spiral of depression and apathy, this will require first awakening the will through exciting encounters and then channeling that will into productive pursuits.

Transmuting Sexual Energy

"Intellectual passion drives out sensuality"

~ Leonardo da Vinci

DaVinci Types have an abundance of sexual/creative energy. This is primarily because DaVincis have very little inherent repression, so sexual/creative impulses are much more likely to reach awareness and they are thus felt more acutely. Once a sexual/creative impulse reaches awareness it can plume like a geyser breaking through the surface – your overall energy system experiences a surge of energy coming up through your spine and through your solar plexus.

Because DaVincis have an abundance of creative energy it is often difficult to find a place to put it all. Sex is an outlet for that. When a DaVinci's creative impulses are stifled or sublimated that energy gets backed up and often feel like an uncontrollable sexual urge. Frustration of this urge can lead to ever escalating energy levels that force the DaVinci mind out of its happy alpha-theta dominance into a beta dominated panic. In this state, DaVincis can be short tempered, harsh, irritable, angry and even rageful. The DaVinci really just needs intimacy, but by this time there is virtually no tenderness in his demeanor and he may even be so frustrated and angry that he can't even fathom allowing the vulnerability of making love.

Sex can also provide the "thrill of the hunt" for a DaVinci if it is to be with a new partner or even with a long-term partner who's being quite playful.

Drugs

There is no doubt that drugs effect brainwave state.

Many stimulants suppress Alpha & Theta waves to produce a greater ratio of Beta wave, but this is a diminished Beta state for DaVincis because it lacks the power and resonance of a true Beta state fully supported by the DaVinci powerhouse of Alpha/Theta brain function. For a DaVinci to be in Beta state without the resonance of their full Alpha/Theta functioning is like playing a violin with white knuckles, singing harshly with no true resonance, or playing golf while gripping the club too tightly.

Ritalin, Tobacco, Caffeine, Yerba Matte, Green Tea and Theanine

Ritalin

Alpha & Theta Brainwaves reduced with Ritalin!

> *"Children exhibiting a positive medication response [to methylphenidate "Ritalin"] had reductions of theta and alpha as well as increased beta in the frontal regions."*

> ~ Department of Psychiatry, University of Colorado Health Sciences Center[8]

Tobacco

Tobacco and Yerba Matte are very similar plants that when ingested have amino acids (similar to Theanine) that encourage Alpha brainwaves.

Athletes use tobacco – and not caffeine for just that reason – tobacco preserves (and even increases) their Alpha/Theta functioning, which is essential for playing in "the zone" – an imperative for achieving greatness in those critical moments.

That's why people smoke cigarettes to "relax." If you are in a Beta brainwave state and you ingest Tobacco, your brainwaves will likely increase in the optimal Alpha zone.

Now there is a significant and often justified cancer scare around tobacco.

Tobacco used to be considered a "healthy" plant – widely used by Native Americans for its psychoactive properties. That was before an industry of American tobacco farmers came about and started messing with the nature of the plant. This industry thrived on cultivating more interesting variations of the once "healthy" tobacco plant by subjecting entire crops to bizarre practices like planting only strains of mutant, sickly, white seeds instead of healthy green ones. These white seeds made "bright" dried tobacco leaves, which had novelty and frou-frou appeal. Later, in the 1950s, big tobacco companies completely contaminated most commercial tobacco with additives like ammonia and isolated nicotine. This apparently enhances the addictive properties of tobacco products. Tobacco is probably one of the most well recorded recent historical examples of how genetic engineering, breeding and tampering can make a once good thing, cancerous.

Another thing American settlers introduced to tobacco consumption was simultaneous alcohol consumption. Using tobacco in conjunction with drinking alcohol seems to cause throat cancer, most likely because drinking alcohol temporarily thins the membranes of the cells of the throat which are then exposed to carcinogens of processed tobacco.

Now, if you're already a smoker, be aware that there are new "additive free" brands out there. American Spirit cigarettes claim to be "100% additive free" so even if they still use the sickly mutant strain of white tobacco, at least you're not inhaling ammonia and 1000 other chemicals along with it. I figure these cigarettes are as bad for people as most other brands (that is *if*, in fact, American Spirit is telling us the truth). The jury is still out on this though.

Caffeine

Caffeine, on the other hand, throws your system into Beta alert/crisis brainwave state. DaVincis using caffeine to "wake up" from their normal Theta functioning will often use stimulants to compensate and wake their systems up. Unfortunately many stimulants over-stimulate your system and throw you out of Theta, past the optimal Alpha state right into the manic/anxiety of Beta state.

Yerba Matte

Yerba Matte is a great alternative. Yerba Matte has a very similar composition to Tobacco, and makes a great tea. It has a more mellow stimulating effect. It will get you out of the dreamy/sleepy Theta state and ease you into the highly creative Alpha state, without the disruptive spike into Beta states.

Green Tea & Theanine

Theanine is an amino acid found in green tea that has been said to be like "zen in a bottle," and its calming effects on brainwave state have been compared to that of tobacco.

In clinical trials, theanine was shown to increase alpha brain waves. And a recent study concluded theanine promotes the generation of alpha-brain waves[9], and promotes relaxation.

Theanine creates a feeling of relaxation and enhances the ability to learn and remember. By reducing worry, theanine appears to increase concentration and focuses thought.

Theanine increases GABA – a brain chemical that is calming and creates a sense of well-being – while on the other hand caffeine decreases GABA. Theanine's ability to increase this brain chemical can literally put you in a better mood. Theanine also increases levels of dopamine –with mood-enhancing effects – which is right where our DRD4 dopamine receptor polymorphism is in effect.

Rock & Roll

Rock – Music

It's no surprise that virtually all rock stars are DaVinci types. Being a genuine rock star requires massive amounts of energy, guts, creativity, spontaneous/impulsive brilliance, and a deep connection with the collective unconscious in order to be "on pulse" with the cutting edge of what the world wants and needs to hear.

Driving rock music tends to be very Alpha state oriented and is great in combination with other Alpha activities like intense athletics or fast driving.

Good music is good for you. Remember to utilize it to restore your brain state to one of harmony and positive energy. Singing or playing an instrument is a great way to get into "the zone" and exercise and increase your power of focus.

Rock – Nature

"Rock" (as in the ones found in nature) – promotes your brain's Alpha-Theta state in a more gentle way. First of all most of nature is in harmony with the Schuman Resonance – the frequency that supported the development of life on this planet, (including your ancestors); so you're automatically going to experience that resonance, which will contribute to your alpha state. Plus the wide open spaces and the fresh air tend to have a calming, centering effect which also can gently guide you into your brain's most sublime frequencies.

Try this: go for a walk on the grass barefoot. Do this for at least 15 minutes and notice how you feel. That's increased Alpha that you'll be experiencing.

Another less involved way to increase your Alpha is to simply be aware of your breathing.

A University of Illinois study found that when ADHD diagnosed children (DaVincis) did activities in natural settings rather than in urban playgrounds they were able to concentrate much better.

Further Recommended Reading:

Last child in the Woods: "Saving Our Children from Nature Deficit Disorder" by Richard Louv

... & Roll – Working Out

Working out, exercising, purging & processing inner demons & past hurts physically is incredibly powerful and beneficial for your temperament. A fellow entrepreneur and reader of The DaVinci Method exclaimed, when I said this to him, "Extensive & strenuous exercise" is a must. It's what keeps us sane. We are genetically wired to need massive amounts of physical activity. This fellow reader is about to embark on a 24 hour non-stop bike ride – a true DaVinci.

Leonardo DaVinci himself was said to wield incredible physical strength, even into his old age. Working out is key to your fulfillment!

For Parents of Young DaVincis

Time and time again, I've been asked. "What do I do with my son who is obviously a DaVinci but can't seem to focus or get along well in school?"

My best advice is this. Every morning before school, take your DaVinci child outside and run them ragged. Get them to run, to sprint, to jump, to yell, to play and be totally free and spontaneous. They need this kind of release, so if you don't help them get it first thing in the morning, they will be trying to get their abundant energy out at "inappropriate" times in their classroom settings. DaVinci children need tons of expansive outdoor physical activity

I know it can be difficult to acquire this new morning ritual of outdoor exercise before school, but it is better than allowing your child to suffer the consequences of having too much energy in a low energy setting like a public school classroom.

You'll find that giving your young DaVinci a high intensity workout each morning allows them to have a much calmer and more focused disposition during those critical classroom hours.

Alpha-Theta Genius

Not all DaVinci types think the same. Some DaVinci types operate from a mainly Alpha brainwave state. Others operate from a mainly Theta brainwave state. This results in vast differences in personality, experience and the kinds of conclusions one derives from those experiences.

The Alpha DaVinci will be much more athletic and outwardly focused. He may not seem so bright – that is intellectually intelligent – but when you get him in a physical situation he'll have an uncanny innate brilliance regarding how he moves his body, the words he chooses, the "actions" he makes. This guy can be a great somatic genius, meaning he's got "it" with regards to his physical presence, communication and coordination

The Theta DaVincis will be much dreamier. He will be the creative genius with potentially a klutzy physical presence. This Theta DaVinci may have learned early on to avoid sports and physical activities, because he is far too lost in thought to be good at athletics. The Theta DaVincis tend to be great artists, inventors and musicians. Sometimes they can be brilliant entrepreneurs, but gaining the respect of their employees can be a challenge because of their lack of outward focus.

Whichever type of DaVinci you identify with more easily, the goal is to find balance. If you are an Alpha DaVinci, you would do well to shift your mind towards that dreamy Theta creativity more often to gain the inspiration that awaits you there. If you are a dreamy Theta type, you would do well to shift towards Alpha to be more present and aware of the outer world and your physical expression with others, so that you can communicate your inspiration into the world.

The ideal center of your consciousness is the Alpha-Theta border. This is at approximately 7.8 Hz – the Schuman Resonance. From here you have access to the inner inspiration available through Theta awareness and the outer charisma and grace of Alpha functioning. But you also gain something much more powerful than just those two functions (Alpha & Theta). When your consciousness is centered on the Schuman Resonance, you come alive! Your mind expands and your energy surges with life. This is the sweet-spot of waking consciousness.

Out of all the different types of brain waves there is a very interesting range called the Alpha-Theta border. This state of mind brings about creativity, intelligence, and a host of other abilities the brain is capable of doing when properly stimulated.

It is a state where the central nervous system reduces input from the peripheral nervous system. The lowering of sensory input serves to normally protect the central nervous system from sensory overload caused by stress or physical damage.

Without these outside functions for the brain to control, the brain expands its functioning powers. The normally unused portion of the brain becomes active and performs at maximum capacity. This range is between 7-8 hertz and this is not so surprising when you learn that the resonant frequency of the earth and ionosphere is approximately 7.5 hertz. Our brains evolved within this dynamic field and used it as a standard to function on. The mind experiences the body in a half-in half-out state of sleep or detachment. The feeling is of being conscious of all things around you but the body being in deep relaxation.

Many cultures discovered this and the methods to achieve this state naturally and artificially. Many of the world's religions were founded on reaching this state and devised strict disciplines to do so. The Alpha-Theta range occurs during reverie, hypnologic imagery, meditation, and by self-hypnosis.[10]

Theta DaVinci Genius Process

People who have the DaVinci Trait have adapted dopamine receptors that cause their brains to resonate at a different frequency than that of the Normal type.

While the Normal type tends to be low in Alpha and Theta brainwaves – giving their waking Beta brainwave state precedence, people who have the DaVinci Trait tend to have brains that are much higher in Alpha and Theta brainwaves sometimes drowning out the more externally focused Beta state brainwaves.

"People with ADD/ADHD … exhibit too much Theta (dreaming) activity. This is the classic inattention for ADD.

With ADHD, hyperactivity keeps people from falling asleep. In essence, the person is combating the high Theta activity and keeping themselves aroused (by increasing their Beta activity)."

~ ADD/ADHD and Biofeedback[11]

What does that mean? What it means is that beta state tends to be a state that of high external attention & alertness, where you are really aware of what is going on outside of you – often at the expense of inner awareness. So when people are in a high beta state, their attention is riveted on what's going on in front of them, they are in a highly attentive state. When they are in an alpha or a theta state, they are more dream-like. They have gone inward, their attention leaps more easily from one thing to the next. It is a low attentive state and, because it is more dreamlike, it is a very creative state.

When people are in the creative place, they tend to seem spacier, sleepier, or not really there. You can picture the mad scientist or the crazy genius who does not even really know his own phone number, but can figure out impossible problems. (Apparently Einstein did not know his own phone number. He said it was because he didn't want to clutter his mind with data that he could find in the phone book.)

What Einstein and Thomas Edison and Leonardo da Vinci all reported doing when they were trying to figure out difficult problems, was they purposefully allowed their minds to drift into Theta states. Edison even had a habit of taking a nap when he was stuck trying to solve a problem. He would let himself drift off and as his mind slipped into Theta state, the answer would flash across his mind and he would wake up with the solution.

Einstein did a very similar thing. Einstein even left clues about how others could do this and what is called "image streaming." What it is, is allowing your mind to drift into the dreamer, less vigilant, less focused state and to watch your mind for what images appear when you're daydreaming. When you're in that place right between awake and asleep and those images start flashing through your mind you can decipher them for clues.

What Einstein told us is that he got many of his answers from those images. When he would have a problem that he's trying to work out but he couldn't figure out – he would realize his conscious mind was working against him in solving the problem – so he would surrender to his deeper wisdom by slipping into Theta state and watching the parade of imagery go by until he got his answer.

"A problem can't be solved with the same thinking that created it."

~ Albert Einstein

Image Streaming

Einstein's way of adjusting his thinking was to allow his mind to go into Theta dream-like states and watch his mind for imagery. It is basically a way of liberating his mind from all of the conscious restraints he has already put on that problem. Now that the problem no longer has the conscious restraints, his unconscious mind can start providing him with all kinds of clues and imagery to the real answer that he is looking for.

If you want to do image streaming, all you need to do is let yourself start daydreaming, maybe close your eyes, and just watch your mind for the images that appear. As you do that, you will receive clues as to whatever problems or concerns are foremost in your consciousness right now.

Image Streaming is a way, especially for DaVinci types, to harness what they are already quite good at. Many DaVinci types have been told most of their lives that they are not being attentive enough, that they are not paying enough attention, and so this natural habit of going into Theta abundant brainwave states over the course of the day while one is supposed to be awake and occupied with their outer activities is a good habit if you are in a profession that involves doing a lot of creative problem solving.

You need to know how to manage your brainwave state, and the way to manage it is to be clear about what state will benefit you the most in any given situation – and then have the discipline to go there.

To solve a problem, the first thing to do is get yourself worked up a bit. You wake yourself up as much as you can. You look at the situation. You say, "Okay, these are the problems I'm trying to solve." You pick one of them, because you do not want to be asking too many questions at the same time.

Once you have gotten your most significant question that you need an answer to right now, frame your question very clearly. Remember you are doing this in the conscious, primarily Alpha or Beta state – the mind states where you have high externalized attention. You look out at the problem. You say, "What are all of the facets of this problem? What are all the qualities of the solution I am hoping for?" You need to be in an externally attentive state so that you are aware of all the stuff the outer world is going to demand of your solution.

Once you've got your problem clear in you mind, then take the question and allow yourself to start daydreaming with that question. Allow yourself to move from an Alpha or Beta brain wave state to a dreamy Theta. As you allow yourself to drift into that dreamlike area of your mind, where you have access to your unconscious mind, (which is far more wise and powerful than your conscious mind), your unconscious will start providing you answers in the form of images.

Then what you need to do, as you are receiving these images, is either to be able to recall what those images are when you come back into your more conscious attentive state, or record yourself just speaking about what you are seeing. Or you could have a friend listen to what you are saying and be able to repeat it back to you. Recording is probably the best because, when you listen back to it, you may find you are giving your conscious self encoded messages in your own words. The words you chose to describe the images you were seeing might actually have clues within them. A friend might paraphrase what you said and thus lose those clues. So, recording is best and that is the second step.

Now with Image Streaming you may get a lot of very strange images that apparently have nothing to do with the problem. That is quite good in fact; because if you are immediately consciously aware of how the images relate to your problem, chances are that you are consciously forcing those images to arise and not actually retrieving them from your unconscious.

Your unconscious mind speaks in riddles. Your unconscious mind speaks in symbols and metaphor. So when your unconscious mind is really the one leading the imagery in your mind, when you are really into that Theta genius state and your unconscious mind has enough of a grasp of the imagery in your mind to lead you toward the answer, you are going to find you are getting a lot of imagery that does not seem to make any sense at all. It will seem strange and bizarre, morphing and dream-like.

What you want to do is record everything you are experiencing there. As you record all of that, what you are giving yourself is a new kind of riddle. A riddle based on your question.

You have already defined the problem as one particular thing, but this new riddle is going to help you redefine the problem and also help you see solutions that may never have occurred to you before. These new solution sets may never have occurred to you if you just stayed in a conscious Beta state. But, as soon as you allow yourself to move into that image-streaming Theta genius state, then you open for yourself the opportunity to gain all kinds of incredibly inspired, intuitive solutions to the problems that you are working with.

Once you have recorded a series of images, come back to your Alpha alert and awake state. Now it's time to perform the second half of making your unconscious solution conscious.

Review all the imagery and apparent messages you have received.

- ▶ What patterns do you notice about the various images, feelings and impressions?

- ▶ What is the overall tone?

- ▶ What does it feel like it is saying?

- ▶ What does it seem to say in the context of the original framing of your problem?

- ▶ What does it seem to suggest about a better way to frame your problem or question?

- ▶ Does anything grab you as a new avenue to explore?

- ▶ Does anything grab you as a warning?

Did you get your unconscious riddle figured out and get solution?

If "yes," Great! You see? You are now are on your way to prolific brilliance.

If "no," not to worry. Now it's time to cycle through again. This time ask your mind to give a riddle that shows you how to solve the first riddle it gave you. Or if that seems too complicated, just ask your mind for another riddle that offers the solution to your problem in a different way. Then let your mind drift back into that dreamy Theta state and repeat this process.

Car Rides on Theta

Car rides on the highway induce an increased Theta brainwave state. It could be the rhythmic sound of wheels turning 50 to 70 mph – creating a Theta brainwave entrainment beat frequency – or it could be the flashes of white dashed dividing line paint whizzing by in a Theta generating frequency. Whatever it is, it'll put your kids to sleep; it'll induce road hallucinations when you're already in low Alpha (i.e. tired); it'll knock you unconscious if you're not careful.

That's the power of external frequencies to affect your mental state. It's good to be aware of this phenomenon, because it is quite powerful. It can also be used to your advantage.

Brainwave Entrainment

Brainwave entrainment is the technical term for the phenomena described above. Brainwave entrainment refers to the brain's response to rhythmic sensory stimulation, such as pulses of light or sound. Knowledge of the properties of brainwave entrainment allows you to intentionally change your mental state by using specific sounds or flashing lights.

Measurements of the EEG (the electrical signals given off by your brain) have led to the finding that brainwave frequencies correspond to specific mental states, which again have been broadly classified into these categories:

Dominant EEG Frequency	Frequency Category	Mental State
15 - 40Hz	Beta	wide awake but jumpy and agitated
10 - 15Hz	High Alpha	alert, wide awake state
8 - 10Hz	Low Alpha	peaceful, contemplative
4 - 8Hz	Theta	meditative, dreamy state
1.5 - 4Hz	Delta	sleep state

You can tell a lot about a person simply by observing their brainwaves. For example, overly anxious people tend to produce an overabundance of high Beta waves while DaVincis (and people with ADD/ADHD) tend to produce an abundance of Alpha and Theta brainwaves.

Researchers have found that brainwaves can be stimulated to change a person's mental state, and even help treat a variety of mental disorders. Brainwave entrainment can even be used to help people access extraordinary experiences such as "lucid dreaming" or amazingly realistic eidetic visualization. (See "DaVincis & Eidetic Imagery" for more on eidetic visualization.)

Stimulating brainwaves with sound

When the brain is given a stimulus, through the ears, eyes or other senses, it emits an electrical charge in response, called a Cortical Evoked Response. When the brain is presented with a rhythmic stimulus, such as a drum beat for example, the rhythm is reproduced in the brain in the form of these electrical impulses. If the rhythm becomes fast and consistent enough, it can start to resemble the brain's natural brainwaves. When this happens, the brain responds by synchronizing its own brainwaves to that same tempo.

Given the right kind of rhythmic stimulation, either through sound or light, your brainwaves can become entrained to the stimulus. If you expose yourself to the right kind of a flashing light or sound with a tempo of 8-10Hz, your brainwave state will eventually become entrained to this stimulus, and you will experience the corresponding peaceful, contemplative Low-Alpha state. Likewise a 4 Hz sound pattern would help reproduce the sleep state in your brain. The same concept can be applied to nearly all mental states, including concentration, creativity and many others. It can even act as a gateway to exotic or extraordinary experiences, such as deep meditation or "lucid dreaming" type states.

To summarize, by using the correct stimulus (light or sound) you can entrain your brainwaves into a desired mental state. This can provide you with an easy high-tech shortcut to help you wake up, focus, relax, meditate, sleep, etc.

Many people have reported that using brainwave entrainment CDs has helped them get out of the vicious cycle of medication: Using caffeine, stimulants (Ritalin, etc.) in the mornings just to get up and alcohol and excessive eating at night just to come down. Instead, many people have found that they can peacefully listen to their High-Alpha CDs in the morning to wake up and feel energized, and then in the evening they can calm themselves and come down just by listening to their Low-Alpha/Theta CDs.

I've prepared a sample brainwave entrainment audio track for you to listen to online and experience what we're talking about here, (plus I've outlined the ideal brainwave therapies for DaVincis). All of this is waiting for you on the web at:

www.DaVinciMethod.com/brainwaves

The Holy Grail

Again, Leonardo DaVinci's mysterious painting The Last Supper, with all of its subtle symbolism, takes on the mystery of the Holy Grail. By removing the expected image of a cup – serving as the sacred chalice of the Holy Grail – Leonardo subtly suggests the true Holy Grail is really something else.

Some have speculated that Mary Magdalene was the Holy Grail carrying on the holy bloodline of Christ, but doesn't that smack of sensationalism? What if the message of The Last Supper is even more sublime? What if all that symbolism is a message from the genius of Leonardo saying, "Look deeply at this union."?

What if The Holy Grail is not some external object to be coveted, (be it a cup or a blood line); but instead an inner state of being – the union of masculine and feminine spirituality? What if the Holy Grail is really inside of you?

Maybe this joining of Mary Magdalene (Symbolizing Eros – feminine divinity) and Jesus (Symbolizing Logos – masculine divinity) is a message to honor both the masculine and feminine approach to God. True genius is being receptive to divine inspiration inwardly (which is a feminine skill), while at the same time capably expressing that divine inspiration outwardly (which is a masculine skill).

Eros, (feminine divinity), correlates to the receptive Theta brainwave state where dreams and visions come to you. Logos, (masculine divinity), correlates to the projective Alpha brainwave state, where your outer movements and communications become most effective. Without Eros (or Theta brainwaves) your actions will lack inspiration and genuine creativity. Without Logos (or Alpha brainwaves) your inspiration lacks effective communication and action.

True divinity has both Eros and Logos. True genius has both Theta and Alpha. Great DaVincis are both receptive to deep intuition and capable of skillfully manifesting that intuitive inspiration into their world. Both feminine receptivity and masculine assertiveness working together make the 'total human', Otto Rank's word for the DaVinci genius.

This perfect state of balance may be reached at the cusp of Alpha-Theta brainwave states, 7.8 Hz which again happens to be in perfect resonance with our planet's electro-magnetic vibration – the seat of life.

"The Goal is Soul!"

Alpha-Theta is where your soul can speak to you. When you are resonating in these regions you will be open to your own soul. When you do something to repress these regions, you will feel disconnected from your soul.

Since your soul is your well-being, when you are in a beta state without a good connection with Alpha-Theta, you will feel anxious and disconnected from well-being.

When you bring yourself into the Alpha-Theta border – the Schuman resonance of the Earth's ionosphere, you will feel a buzz of resonance with all life. Clarity will befall you, because you are now in harmony with the wavelength that cultivated all life on this planet – and binds it to this day.

I have come to know this also as the buzz of truth, because, (like goose-bumps or a chill up your spine), I receive this experience when I am experiencing a profound truth.

DaVincis think in Wholes

*"The part always has a tendency to reunite with
its whole in order to escape from its imperfection."*

~ Leonardo da Vinci

DaVincis (especially Theta oriented DaVincis) tend to think in wholes, because their consciousness rests so closely to the holistic (and total) sea of the unconscious. The unconscious mind thinks totally – not in parts. It "groks" (to steal some slang from the 60s) everything.

The conscious mind – especially while trapped by the ego – is *defined* by its partialness. It is just a tiny "part" of the whole mind. It is just a dot on the vast ocean of the total unconscious mind. It is even symbolized with the mere 5% of the brain that is activated by the ego.

So, DaVincis tend to be "big picture" people – where they recognize everything as related. They prefer to give "all or nothing." They run hot or cold. They are often referred to by Otto Rank as the "total human" because of this characteristic.

You'll note that DaVinci types (again especially the more Theta oriented ones) are slower to speak, because they are formulating their thoughts from the great wholeness of being.

On the other hand the Normal type is much quicker on the surface, is prone to running almost exclusively on cultural programming (because this is what Beta brainwaves elicit in the brain), and is more comfortable thinking in parts and giving partially.

Life in this society demands continuous partialization, and the Normal type is well adjusted to living by a continuous partial paying off, without wanting to give or to preserve his whole being undivided in any experience. This, however, is the primary endeavor the DaVinci type – the 'total human' – whom often succeeds in carrying through his totality creatively, but also, is frequently shattered neurotically in the attempt.

While we protect ourselves with rules, ideals, codes and restrictions from too quick living out or living up, we feel ourselves guilty of this unused life.[12]

This taken to a broader context makes up the laws, customs and cultural norms, which have over generations proven to provide the 'average man' with a scheme of which he is glad to make use, while the 'total human' type has difficulties fitting in to this partial living.

90% Do 20% – You Do 100%

"Do or do not. There is no 'try'."
~ Yoda (definitely a DaVinci)

One thing to recognize, for all you DaVinci types, is that you tend to operate at zero to 10% of your ability or 90–100%. You're black or white. You're hot or cold. This isn't normal by our societal standards.

Societal norms tend to be determined by the 90 percent of our population that does not have the DaVinci trait. Those who are not the DaVinci type tend to work well with partials. They tend to operate well on 20 or 30 percent of their potential and the reason that they work well that way is because they're genetically designed to work well that way. But you're not.

Think about this: the last 10,000 years or so our world has been dominated by agriculture, by farming. What has been naturally selected as the most desirable personality temperament in many situations is the humble, slow, and steady farmer. That farmer isn't supposed to use himself up all at once in a fast spurt. The farmer is meant to operate at 20 to 30 percent of his physical threshold all day, day in and day out, all year long – and that's how the crops get taken care of on a regular basis. Methodically and regularly, that's how the farming chores get done.

Now the DaVinci type is different. DaVincis are valuable in a different way. DaVinci types really work more like the hunter archetype. The hunter is one who for most of the time is lounging around, enjoying the community, the family, the children, having spiritual journeys and then for maybe one to four hours a day goes hunting. Even then those few hours of hunting are mostly filled with leisurely travel on foot looking for the prey until one finds what they're hunting for and then all-of–the sudden in the flash of an instant the hunter goes full bore into 100% physical exertion. Sprinting, spearing, and capturing that night's dinner.

You can figure on any given day a hunter is maybe at 100 percent for no more than an hour and then the rest of the day is really about leisure at somewhere between zero and ten percent of the hunter's physical potential.

What you need to realize about this difference is that when you work with people, nine out of ten people are going to expect you to operate consistently at 20 to 30 percent, which is outside of your range. You don't operate on those levels and when you try to what you are really doing is oscillating between ten percent and 100 percent very quickly and trying to get that balance so that you look like you're giving 30 percent just like everybody else. That is incredibly draining for you, because that's just not how you were designed to work.

You may become very frustrated working with people who expect long durations of 20-30% effort from you, because that's not how you operate. You'll either be bored out of your mind or you'll be creating some sort of mischief that allows you the opportunity to get back up to that 100% level.

Now, the reciprocal of that can occur when people are working for you. You need to determine whether they are DaVinci types or Normal types. Because if they are Normal types they're only going to give you 20% when you want 100%, and they'll be confused and irritated when between those 100% emergency bursts you're letting everyone play and lounge around in preparation for that next emergency.

Maybe 30% is their absolute maximum and you're going to expect that these Normal type people – at the drop of a dime – are going to be able to turn on a 100% super-heroic performance for you. When they don't deliver, you're going to be very frustrated with them. You're going to think "What is wrong with you people?! Can't you give 100 percent?! I know you can do better than that!" They consistently won't and it'll drive you nuts – and you'll drive them nuts.

Normal types working for you will be thinking, "This guy's brilliant but he's nuts. He wants too much out of us. I do consistently decent work when I'm in a stable environment. I don't like all this emergency!" But that's how you operate. Emergencies are when you are at your best.

You like to perform at 100% or you don't like to perform at all. You're hot or cold, off or on. You need to know this about yourself. You need to know this about the people that you work with. If they're a 20 to 30 percent Normal type, which nine out of ten times they're likely to be, then what you need to do is honor that in them and put them in positions where they're insulated from your oscillations and the oscillations of the market. Don't put them in a place where you're going to expose them to some emergency and expect them to be able to turn themselves on at 100 percent. They just don't do that – and it'll drive you both crazy if you try to get them to do that. This kind of misunderstanding of co-worker's operating thresholds can create a lot of discontent.

Team Up With Other DaVinci Types

You might need a couple of the DaVinci types to work with you so that when you do have those 100% emergency opportunity times – when you say "Okay guys, now's our big chance. Now we really need to go for it!" Other DaVinci types will actually be ready to go at 100%. You've got to have your 100% team of DaVinci types so you can do that. It's a different team. It's a different mentality and when you're clear about who's a DaVinci type and who's a Normal type you can be very effective about who you use to go into battle with.

When I say "go into battle" I mean when you have an opportunity that needs 100% from people. You know your 100% team and you go into battle with that 100% team. Then you need to know who are your slow and steady farmers that will help you keep an even keel during the times when you're lounging around at your zero or ten percent. Both qualities can work very well in an organization provided you know how to use each type towards their strengths. Then you will have a great team.

100% Jerk Behaviors

Because you, as a DaVinci, operate at 0 or 100% and you expect that from everyone else, you'll often interpret a Normal type's 20 – 30% contribution as insufficient and regard it as you would regard your own 0% state. That means a Normal type will appear to a DaVinci to always be in their relaxed state and never fully "stepping up to the plate." When a DaVinci counts on this Average person, the DaVinci may start exhibiting the 100% Jerk Behaviors listed below. (Incidentally these Behaviors have been playfully labeled Retention Deficit Disorder by Dr. Beverly Kaye, a business talent retention expert, which shows unconscious awareness that

these behaviors are most often perpetrated by leaders with ADD –
that is, neurotic DaVinci types.)

100% Jerk Behaviors

- ✓ Demanding
- ✓ Lacking Patience
- ✓ Blowing Up
- ✓ Criticizing
- ✓ Withholding Praise
- ✓ Setting Impossible Deadlines
- ✓ Not Listening
- ✓ Not Caring
- ✓ Distrusting
- ✓ Blaming
- ✓ Breaking Promises
- ✓ Giving Mostly Negative Feedback

As you endeavor to heal these tendencies in yourself, first
you would do well to ask:

How are you a jerk to yourself?

How can you forgive yourself for the things your jerk side
judges?

You can try saying "I forgive myself for judging myself for
[INSERT JERK BEHAVIOR]." to disarm this jerk-judgment cycle.
Meaning you are clarifying that it is not the "inadequacy" that needs
forgiving but your act of judgment that really needs forgiving.

Relating to Your World as a Whole

*"There are people who appear to think only with
the brain ... While others think with all the body
and all the soul, with the blood, with the marrow
of the bones, with the heart, with the lungs, with
the belly, with the life."*

~ Unamuno

By acknowledging everything as symbolic we bridge the gap between the partial and the whole. Each partial thing is a symbolic expression of the entire whole that contains it.

You can relate to each part of your world wholly and completely through symbolism, this is your bridge into genius, because your entire mind can be activated this way.

Learn to see the universe as holographic. Every little detail contains all the information you need about the whole. The devil's in the details, but so is God. When you try to take too much into account at once you blind yourself to what's right in front of your nose – everything symbolized in one holographic glimpse.

Synchronicity

*"A man of genius makes no mistakes; his errors
are volitional and are the portals of discovery."*

~ James Joyce

Synchronicity means a coincidence of events that seem related but are not obviously caused one by the other.

The Butterfly Effect

Once you begin to notice the holographic nature of your world, you will see all sorts of seemingly unrelated occurrences become fused together by invisible webs of causality. The smallest detail will have the greatest power to shape future events. The most disparate occurrences will ring with resonance and point your mind towards deeper solution that uproots the deeper imbalances at play. You will see a small detail out of place and you will begin to recognize that your unconscious mind is showing you that detail for a purpose, that there is something powerful in that detail.

The Butterfly Effect is a law of chaos theory. Originally pioneered by a meteorologist, the theory goes like this:

A massive level 5 hurricane, the kind that can swiftly obliterate entire expanses of the U.S. Atlantic coastline, could be "caused" or set in motion by something as seemingly insignificant as the puff of air from a butterfly's fluttering wings on the Africa coastline, provided that butterfly is in just the right place at just the right time.

No deed is insignificant, no detail irrelevant, no awareness negligible, no act of kindness unimportant.

If you notice something, no matter how seemingly insignificant – pay attention to that, for your unconscious mind is showing you something – there is a purpose to your noticing that detail in that moment. There is method to your madness.

The dilemma is that you don't know what any deed will actually lead to, you don't always know what is truly right or kind.

That is where prayer comes in. It is only an Intelligence that knows how your actions will affect everything for all time that could possibly lead you to actually "do the *right* thing." With this awareness I offer you this simple prayer that has worked well for me:

"I am here only to be truly helpful.

I am here to represent God Who sent me.

*I do not have to worry about what to say or what
to do, because God Who sent me will direct me.*

*I am content to be wherever God wishes; knowing
God goes there with me.*

I am healed as I let God teach me to heal."[13]

~ Adapted from **A Course in Miracles**

This prayer will help you align your intentions with a higher purpose and it will remind you who you are choosing to represent in your encounters. You may find that you are much more graceful in your encounters with people when you are clear that it is your intention to represent the love of God, rather the petty needs of your ego in that moment.

Bono has said that he finds great steadfastness when he is personally petitioning Presidents and Heads of State for his campaign to erase the injustice of Africa's debt, because he believes when he walks through their doors he is doing it as an ambassador for God's will.

This simple thought can open you to the assistance of miracles.

Looking in Wholes

*"Genius is the ability to see things invisible,
to manipulate things intangible,
to paint things that have no features"*

~ Joseph Joubert

Your entire unconscious mind surrounds you. Look at your world. Look at your immediate surroundings. This is truly the content of your unconscious, because you can only see what your unconscious holds and binds with meaning.

The world makes no sense. It appears as random, but it is simply too often beyond your conscious ability to grasp. For example, what do see in this string of numbers: (120,158) (177,46) (203,166) (111,86) (230,97)?

Did you see just meaningless numbers? Or did you see a star? The first pair of numbers (120,158) are the xy coordinates of the starting point. A line is then drawn to the second pair of xy coordinates (177,46), then to the third pair of xy coordinates

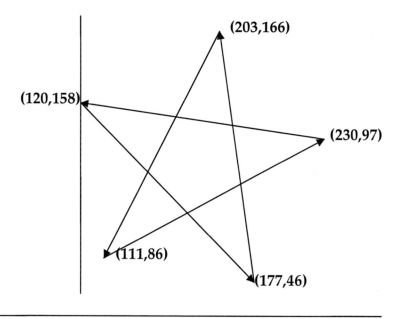

(203,166), and so on, to create the five-pointed star shape.

Your unconscious mind probably would have shown you a star (or something symbolizing a star), had you instead allowed your unconscious to show you what it already knows. This can be done using the process of **image streaming**. Because your unconscious mind is so much vaster and more transcendently powerful than your conscious mind, it can literally see how everything relates – this offers a virtual 50,000 foot view of your life and your world.

So, if you ask you unconscious mind to "connect the dots" for the events, experiences and synchronicities in your life, you may discover you are being shown something much grander and more meaningful than a disparate sequence of occurrences.

> *"By acknowledging everything as symbolic we bridge the gap between the partial and the whole. Each partial thing is a symbolic expression of the whole."*
>
> ~ Garret LoPorto

"Pay attention to this."

Synchronicity plays in our lives like a symphony showing what it is we need to see. Synchronicity whispers in your ear, "Pay attention to this."

Alas, we tend to pay attention to more than the actual content of the clue. The alarming experience of another unexplainable coincidence captures our attention and eclipses the actual message.

A synchronistic event is best peacefully acknowledged, egolessly. Each synchronicity reveals the content of the healing immediately available to us. It is a clue, not a fact. It is a means, not an end. It is an effect, not a cause. Follow the clue to discover a deeper prejudice holding you prisoner from within your own mind. It is your opportunity to let go of this prejudice.

What are you being offered to forgive? What have you been unwilling to admit, to accept, to learn up until now? What are you willing to accept gracefully now – that only a moment before might have thrown you. The synchronicity is an invitation to heal further along the way shown. However, it still requires egoless wisdom to help you to interpret your synchronicity accurately.

Pain is the gift of the ego. When you are in pain, you have chosen the wrong teacher. Your Spirit is accompanied in joy. Choose joy first, then deliberate over your dilemmas. When you have turned to your soul, you will spontaneously recognize the perfect next note to play in the magnificent symphony of joy that surrounds us.

Synchronicity– In & Out of Your Mind

I believe the word "synchronicity" was coined by Carl Jung, in an attempt to describe the occurrence of events both within one's mind and outside of one's mind at the same time.

If you're thinking about something and then you notice some strange coincidence in the world around you that reflects that thought, that would be synchronicity. It's a clue that you're thinking in line with your unconscious or preconscious.

Synchronicity can be really helpful when you have a clear intention within you. When you have a clear desire or purpose, you will find that there are many coincidences outside of you that will reinforce your ability to accomplish that desire or purpose. That clarity of thought and intention within you can be manifested outside of you in ways that you would think would have be impossible to control – things that are much bigger than your physical influence.

This synchronistic dance can coalesce in ways that allow you to take shortcuts towards your goal. Maybe you have a goal to do a project that involves making a connection with someone of importance. You have no idea how you would ever be in touch with him but you have a very clear intention that you want to do this project and that person is going to need to be involved in order for you to accomplish your goal. You may find, as your intention becomes stronger and clearer, coincidences – serendipities – appear, which bring you closer to making that connection. They give you shortcuts to having that connection with that person.

This also hits on the idea of "six degrees of separation." There is a theory that you are connected to every person on the planet by no more than six relationships, so that if you knew just the right six relationships to work through, you'd be able to be in contact with whoever you want to be in contact with on the planet. You just have to know which six relationships; which can become very complicated. But something like synchronicity can help you with that.

Now, see, the appropriate usage of synchronicity as far as I can tell, is to help you move toward your highest good and to give you feedback about where you are coming from. For instance, if you keep bumping into the same kinds of people with the same kinds of issues, you can be pretty certain that you *too* share those same issues and the reason you keep running into others with your issues is to give you an opportunity to heal that issue through your encounter with them.

Synchronicity always starts inside of you with your inner intentions. So, you need to be very clear on what your purpose is, and to make sure that your purpose is in alignment with your soul's deeper desires, with your own spiritual values, with what is true and good because you can just as easily have synchronicity with egotistical purposes that lead you into circles of others with those same ego drives.

You could want something and you could start manifesting coincidences that'll help you have that something that you want. There's a whole culture around the idea that, if you want something and you start seeing coincidences around that wanting, it must be pre-destined to be a good thing; that you *must* be on your spiritual path because you've wanted something and now you are seeing coincidences that seem to be availing you of what you want. However, this is not necessarily true.

Coincidences and synchronicity around what you are wanting, does not mean it is really the best thing for you. It just means that you want it enough that you are manifesting these coincidences. So, the proper thing, the thing to be aware of is that whatever you want, whatever you choose to do, whatever intentions you hold inside of you, will in some way be attracted to you. The more powerfully you are aligned with what your deepest values and desires are, the more powerfully you will enjoy the happy luck of synchronicity.

Because you are a DaVinci and have a greater conscious connection with your unconscious desires, you will likely manifest much more in the way of synchronicities. Also because you are a DaVinci who is often looking at the big picture – taking a holistic view of things and seeing in wholes – you are much more likely to notice synchronicities. And finally because you are a DaVinci who is more prepared to follow a spontaneous impulse – willing to turn on a dime – you are more likely to use synchronicities to your advantage.

Got Devotion?
Know "What for?"
& Honor Your Priorities.

"Obstacles cannot crush me.
Every obstacle yields to stern resolve.
He who is fixed to a star
does not change his mind."

~ Leonardo da Vinci

Part of the human condition seems to be a compulsive unwillingness to prioritize well. We all focus our energy on so many things, but it seems we continually neglect what matters most.

Successful DaVincis don't become preoccupied too early with concrete methods and tactics. They realize those are just secondary decisions. The primary choice is "What's the purpose?"

I remember whenever I used to share my cockamamie "it'll be HUGE and we'll make tons of money" business ideas with Ben of Ben & Jerry's. He would always remind me in his friendly slow voice, "Soooooo – What for?" and I would immediately become aware once again of the guiding principle he always held: Having a greater social good is the guiding purpose of any worthwhile endeavor.

Holding to this one principle is clearly more valuable to him than getting riches without it. Yet, he has become quite wealthy *because* of his clarity of purpose, his choice to remain undistracted by "the fast buck" and his willingness to experiment wildly while getting where he truly wants to be.

To clearly hold an intentionally chosen vision while experimenting with many ways to make that vision a reality has much power. With a clear and firmly held vision you can overcome the distractions that get so many of us off course.

Without a clear purpose in mind you might spend most of your time and energy on urgent, unimportant distractions instead of going for your true goal. Distractions can even take on a life of their own and preoccupy you with shallow fixations like, "I want tons of money, fast." in lieu of your true goals, which are probably closer to, "I want to bring great value and life into this world."

What is The Purpose of Your Life?

"What we fear is not death.
What we fear is that we have wasted life.
In our darkest moments we are afraid that our
highest calling will go unanswered."

~ Garret LoPorto

To know the deepest purpose of your life is to know clearly where to put your focus. When you clearly know your purpose you find it easy to say "no" to everything else and to move forward ruthlessly towards the accomplishment of your life's highest goals.

> *"This will be our response to violence: to make music more intensely, more beautifully, more devotedly than ever before."*

> ~ Leonard Bernstein

A true devotion will set you free. A true devotion will fill your heart and fuel your day. For a DaVinci, great devotion is the only path to true success.

With Great Devotion, nothing is "failure." It's all "learning" & "practice."

> *"A baseball player who misses two out of three times is deemed to be one of the most successful batters ever."*

> ~ Russell Bishop

In the same year Babe Ruth hit more home runs than any player in the history of baseball, he also struck out more times than any other player. In the same year that Michael Jordan scored more points than any other basketball player in the NBA, he also missed more shots than any other player.

Successful venture capitalists have a saying, "fail fast." They understand that 9 out of 10 businesses fail. They also understand that the 1 out of 10 that actually succeeds will make them rich. So the adage "fail fast" means get through the failures as quick as possible so you have time for more successes.

> *"If I had to do it all over again,*
> *I'd make the same mistakes ... only sooner."*

You are like Babe Ruth and Michael Jordan (both DaVinci types) so get used to it. Taking more wild swings allows you to make more home runs. Taking more shots helps you make more baskets. Risking more failures is what gives you the opportunity to have more successes.

Edison thought it would take just a few weeks to invent the bulb, but it ended up taking him almost two years of "misses" before he reached his goal. It's said he tried over 6,000 different carbonized plant fibers, looking for a carbon filament for his light bulb.

> *"Genius is one percent inspiration*
> *and ninety-nine percent perspiration."*

~ Thomas Alva Edison

A Clear Higher Purpose + Taking Risks = Eventual Success

Thomas Edison's purpose was not just to get a single bulb to light up, but to light up the whole world with this invention. By focusing on the higher intention of inventing an entire lighting system rather than just a single light bulb (with a willingness to keep taking risks and trying things), Edison succeeded where others failed.

Edison's choice helped him invent an entire lighting system including wiring, plugs, connectors, and such that could be used to light thousands of bulbs, not just one. This is largely why he is given credit for inventing the light bulb (while others had similar claims), because it was his inventions that gave the world a way to actually *use* his light bulb – which was his clear higher purpose.

Life and death

Otto Rank also introduced the idea of the inner psychic struggle between life and death. He said we have a "**life instinct**" that propels us to become individuals, competent and independent, and a "**death instinct**" that retreats us back into the womb to be part of a family, community, or humanity.

We also experience fear of both life and death. The "**fear of life**" is the fear of separation, loneliness, and alienation; the "**fear of death**" is of getting lost in the whole, slipping into oblivion, losing our special identity in the great oneness of being.

Rank's earliest work concerned **birth trauma**, which is a reminder of the horror of our original separation from God. Our subsequent lives are filled with separations, beginning with this birth trauma. After birth, there's weaning, potty training, discipline and work, judgment and heartbreaks … But to avoid these separations is, literally, to avoid life and choose death – never facing the inner horror of separation squarely, never finding out what you are capable of, never leaving your family, your mother, your comfort zone, or the womb. You must shed all of these to become the Artist.

Then to face the death fear you must shed all the beliefs that make up the original wounds that shaped your ego – and face the oblivion of the self you created to protect you from the horror of the separation.

So you must face your fears, recognizing that, to be fully developed, you must embrace both the separation of "life" and the relinquishment of your separation in "death."

The Fear of Death – the Fear of Goals

To make anything a definite GOAL is to destroy its appeal to the neurotic DaVinci type:

*"For the goal is an end
and the end is death for the neurotic."*

~ Otto Rank[14]

The fear of goals is a primary trouble for DaVincis. We can see how this trouble plagued Leonardo da Vinci. He barely finished anything he began – but when he did actually finish something, how amazing it was.

Completion = Death symbolically. This doesn't bother the Normal type so much because each completion is seen as just a tiny partial death – no big deal. However to the Theta DaVinci type – who experiences life in wholes – each completion can loom like oblivion and the total fear of death may accompany this end. Often because of this total death fear, a DaVinci will do everything in their power to abort the total completion of something.

"Art is never finished, only abandoned."

~ Leonardo da Vinci

The act of putting out, which the Artistic DaVinci type perceives rightly – not only as a birth but also as a dying – the neurotic DaVinci can bring to pass in no way. He only takes in, he gives nothing out. He seeks to complete his ego constantly at the cost of others without paying for it.[15]

Because the neurotic DaVinci type, refuses to give his energy completely to his tasks, he becomes inwardly dissociative splitting off islands of this left over psychic energy. These islands of unused psychic energy – stolen from their proper expression – serve as a secret life reserve for that dark hour – the moment of death – in the delusional subconscious plan that one could hoard life and extend it this way. So instead of being fully alive and engaged in their present life the neurotic DaVinci type will indulge in oversleeping, overeating and over-relaxing (in its various forms, which include sex, alcohol, drugs and procrastination) in order to stave off the fear of death for awhile, by believing he is making deposits into a life extending reserve, but this reserve does not exist.

> *"Somebody should tell us, right at the start of our lives, that we are dying. Then we might live life to the limit, every minute of every day. Do it! I say. Whatever you want to do, do it now! There are only so many tomorrows."*

~ Pope Paul VI quotes (Italian Pope. 1897-1978)

The typical neurotic DaVinci is an individual who kills off a part of his being – reminiscent of an ancient sacrificial killing in order to protect himself from retaliation from the Gods for being a coward and contributing less than he could be. In doing this, he has made himself incapable of living.

Your opportunity as a self aware DaVinci is to confront this horrible death fear head on. To recognize, in every little thing that symbolizes incompleteness in your life, that you can fearlessly face your mortality through its completion and by doing so set more of your being free.

With each completion, you will be rewarded for your bravery with massive releases of energy, vitality, creativity and joy. This is the boon of your heroic journey. Do this often enough and you will be rewarded with great wealth, health and happiness.

> *"Genius begins great works; labor alone finishes them."*

~ Joseph Joubert

As you progress through the agony of completion, experiencing the thrilling release of putting each incomplete project to rest, you will probably learn to only start what you intend to finish, because suffering through the completion of something you never really wanted is a most horrendous fate.

"The true genius shudders at incompleteness - and usually prefers silence to saying something which is not everything it should be."

~ Edgar Allan Poe

The final relic of the fear of death and completion is the wakening of your inner awareness of what each completion tells you about the way you have spent your precious life. When you avoid completing something you can avoid the awareness of what its eventual completion may tell you about you. What if it's not "good" enough? What if it shows I'm incompetent? What if it is not – in the end – the work of genius of which I am capable? Will I not be remembered by the mediocrity of this completion?!

"I have offended God and mankind because my work didn't reach the quality it should have."

~ Leonardo da Vinci

To master completion, you must begin by taking your self (your ego), your creations and your death much less seriously. When you don't take your self seriously, completion becomes easy because what you lose by its completion (your legacy and your life) is not seen as so important.

When you stop taking your self seriously, you will stop defending against its demise and in that relinquishment of defense you will become intimately aware of the graceful impermanence of every aspect of life. This will liberate you to enjoy the moment and complete your goals without anxiety.

"If you realize that all things change, there is
nothing you will try to hold on to.
If you are not afraid of dying,
there is nothing you cannot achieve."

~Unknown

Finally, incompletion in the face of death is a waste of life. You are given life to complete its purpose. When you hesitate or retreat from the opportunities to live up your life fully, you will experience the intolerable guilt of wasting life. It is this guilt that will weigh you down and drain your zest for life – because now in order to reach each new experience of being truly alive you must first be faced with the guilt of having rejected your previous opportunities to fully live life. You are thus caught in a lifeless holding pattern – devoid of vitality or enthusiasm – until you can overcome the guilt of your earlier wasted moments of life.

This guilt may look like anger or hurt or resentment, but it is – underneath it all – guilt for having not been the greatest expression of you, of your soul in a previous moment. You must cast off this buried guilt and meet this moment anew, throw all your being into your *present* opportunity to express the greatness of your soul.

"As a well spent day brings happy sleep,
so a life well spent brings happy death."

~ Leonardo da Vinci

This principle has been described in religion as guilt or karma. Guilt in Christianity leads to purgatory – if it is resolvable – and Hell if it is not. The resolvable guilt can be processed over in purgatory by reliving those "fallen" moments. In eastern religion, the Karmic Wheel is a way of describing the principle of having to complete and resolve each moment you have wasted in life – only you keep coming back to this world (being reincarnated) again and again until it is accomplished.

Whichever belief system you subscribe to, the message is this: You are here to live up your life so totally that your eventual death becomes a happy respite.

"The goal of all life is death."

~ Sigmund Freud

Procrastination & Completion

"It's easier to resist at the beginning
than at the end."

~ Leonardo da Vinci

Here's another reason why you procrastinate. You have experienced the power of your spontaneous insights to render useless all you have struggled to do, because these insights reveal short-cuts and offer questions you never thought to ask. You could struggle for hours searching your house for your wallet only to discover it's been in your back pocket the whole time. It is the spontaneous insight that reminds you where your wallet is, so why bother doing all that searching in the first place?

You could spend weeks on a project, pursuing a particular approach only to discover in one momentary flash of insight that all you have done can be completely transcended in a single move. If you had just looked at the project from this new perspective, right in the beginning, you could have done the project better and done it in days instead of weeks. So why start the project in the first place?

For example: You could struggle years (or decades!) saving every penny to reach the goal of having a million dollars, or you could reach that same goal in just a few short months with just one brilliant idea.

For DaVinci types, brilliant ideas come easily and suddenly when we're open to them. Take Alex Tew's story for example:

"It was a muggy summer's night late in August (2005), the time around midnight, and there I was, lying on my bed with a notepad, brainstorming ideas to make money for [college]. I think I'm quite a creative person, so I wanted to come up with an idea that was unique and would hopefully capture people's imagination, but with the whole purpose of making money. No point being shy about it! I think we brits can sometimes be too shy about money. Well bugger that, I DO NOT want to be a broke student!

So anyway, after an hour of two of jotting random things on paper, the idea seemingly popped out of nowhere. Almost like my subconscious mind had been ticking over in the background, working it all out. So it just kind of happened. That's about it. I scribbled it down and within about 10 minutes a picture of what needed to be done had emerged."

Alex's idea was to make a simple homepage with a million pixels on it and sell advertising space on it for a $1 per pixel. He called it The Million Dollar Homepage. Four months later Alex's crazy little idea had made him a million dollars with very little effort.

Alex could have done what others do when they need money for school. He could have just got himself a job. But then, he'd probably be a million dollars poorer if he did. By not getting right to work on the project of making some money for school, but instead taking some focused time to let his unconscious mind give him the best solution, Alex used "procrastination" to his advantage.

No wonder you choose to procrastinate! Why struggle to do anything, when you know there's a good chance a powerful revelation will come to you during the process and show you a completely different and better way to accomplish what you set out to do? Why let yourself be blindsided by another one of your revelations? Why not just relax and enjoy yourself with other distractions while you wait for it to come?

"I'm just distracting myself from waiting."

~ My 5 year old son John

Here's an important distinction: Alex was disciplined enough to use his "procrastination" time to really focus on the problem and allow his mind to come up with many possible solutions until he stumbled upon something captivatingly brilliant. Then he had the passion to act on that brilliant idea immediately.

Often us DaVinci types have trouble getting enough motivation to focus like that. We're too good at ignoring our own problems until they become disasters. So often what is missing is the motivation and energy and focus to really think about our projects in the first place.

A great remedy to this lack of focus is to immediately engage in the initial struggle of doing your project the old fashioned way, while keeping clear in your mind, "there has got to be a better way." The sheer contrast between your current experience of drudgery, and your knowledge that there's probably some brilliant solution to your problem – which would render completely useless everything you are toiling with – will at very least motivate your mind to stay focused on finding that transcendently, "better way."

Sometimes your initial struggle *is* the *key* to unlocking your great revelations! Without your struggle, your mind has no impetus to provide you with the revelation.

"I have wasted my hours."

~ Leonardo da Vinci

So yes, being a DaVinci, at sometime during the completion of your project, you will likely be struck with an amazing insight into the nature of your project that completely topples all of your previous concepts and plans for it. You will want to start your project from scratch in this better, completely new way. Realizing this, at least subconsciously, you used to think something along the lines of

"Why bother beginning now, then? Why not just wait for that spectacular insight and then begin. Won't that save me a great deal of struggle?" The answer is "no!"

The only way you get to have that amazing insight, that paradigm shift of thought, that out of the box solution, is to *engage* in your project – *encounter* the frustrating complexities of your current approach to achieving its goals. Only through this impetus, only by way of this payment to the gods of your awareness, may your conscious mind grow tired of relying on its own struggling meekness, and may your unconscious mind offer the reward, the elixir to your struggle.

> *"Everything you want is out there waiting for you*
> *to ask. Everything you want also wants you. But*
> *you have to take action to get it."*
> *~ **Jules Renard***

Alternating Struggle & Rest

> *"Men of lofty genius when they are doing the least*
> *work are most active."*
>
> ~ Leonardo da Vinci

Your greatest breakthroughs will occur when your mind is quiet. It is then that the subtle whisper of fate can lead your awareness to your next great advance. However, this privilege must be earned with the sweat of your brow. These subtle hints only come to a truly quiet mind and a truly quiet mind is often only won after a satisfying struggle with your situation. Once your ego's habitual tactics are sufficiently exhausted, your mind will relax and fall open to a greater wisdom.

One way to experience this phenomenon is to exercise to the point of exhaustion and immediately after you finish your exercise, lay down on the floor and let your mind drift. It is at this time that you will experience greater clarity.

"It takes a lot of time to be a genius,
you have to sit around so much doing nothing,
really doing nothing."

~ Gertrude Stein

So it is with the subtle hints of genius that come from your deep and powerful unconscious. They are only recognizable to one who has asked the hard questions and exhausted the confines of all his preconceptions around a particular problem. For only after one has thrown themselves against the wall too many times for the arrogance of the ego to sustain itself, does one tend to surrender his pride and truly invite divine aid.

*"When I am weak, then **am** I strong."*

~ 2nd Corinthians 12:10

So it is that great victories and breakthroughs are won first by the force of struggle, then by the enlightened receptivity of true rest.

This is how the muscle strengthens itself, struggle then rest, struggle then rest.

"Every now and then go away, have a little
relaxation, for when you come back to your work
your judgment will be surer. Go some distance
away because then the work appears smaller and
more of it can be taken in at a glance and a lack of
harmony and proportion is more readily seen."

~ Leonardo da Vinci

The Power of Hyper-focus

*"As every divided kingdom falls,
so every mind divided between many studies
confounds and saps itself."*

~ Leonardo da Vinci

Once you have struggled and then rested, allowing inspiration to conceive itself in your mind, you will gain the impetus to give 100% of your being to the manifestation of that inspiration.

When Leonardo would finally engage in his work; he would lock-on. "When he was working, he would rise before dawn, climb the scaffolding and paint from sunrise to sunset; the brush never leaving his hand. More often than not, he would forget to eat and drink. – Then he might do no work at all for 2 or 3 days, carefully examining the work he had done." "On some days he would take his brush, paint one or two strokes, and then suddenly leave."

~ Monteau Bondello (recalling Leonardo da Vinci painting the Last Supper)

You, as a DaVinci type, have the amazing ability to "lock-on" to a task and hyper-focus on it until it is done. This super-human level of focus and determination comes rarely, but when it comes – watch out there is nothing that can stand in your way.

*"Thou, O God, dost sell us all good things
at the price of labor"*

~ Leonardo da Vinci

Cooperate with me or Die!

Because the DaVinci type sees in wholes, and thus sees how everyone can work seamlessly and interdependently, he is naturally cooperative and thus has a genius for mediating conflict and moving towards harmony. The DaVinci – Mathematical Genius and Nobel Laureate John Nash (featured in "A Beautiful Mind") – showed how a DaVinci can even use math to express his profound longing for deep human interdependence and cooperation to be realized.

Also because the Theta DaVinci deals almost exclusively in wholes, and almost never in partials, competition becomes all-or-nothing – we are either cooperative and in harmony as 'one' or we are deeply separate and in mortal combat as competitors. Thus competition is either fierce or not at all – while for Average or 'partial' types, competition can be a very limited and pleasant play with a tiny fragment of the death wish.

To the Theta DaVinci type, the concept of competition is so unnatural that if ingested and assimilated too deeply in their subconscious is deeply destructive. It results in a splitting off of their mind into fragments and fuels neurosis and dissociative disorders. On the less extreme end of the spectrum, this deep seated fear of competition creates massive anxiety around any perceived areas of separation in their life. Separation is any area where you feel your interests and those of others diverge.

Remember that you run hot or cold with your perceptions, because you perceive in wholes. So when you see someone as being "with you", you experience great closeness to them. But when you see someone as "separate and against you" that against-ness saturates your every perception of that person so thoroughly that you begin to see them as "evil".

Ultimately, the only thing that's really evil is the belief that others are truly separate from you. Consequently, by holding to the conviction that you and your adversary are the same; you can heal almost any relationship.

DaVincis are Dreamers

*"The future belongs to those who believe
in the beauty of their dreams."*

~ Eleanor Roosevelt

Listen to Your Soul

There are three aspects to your consciousness. There's the personality, there's the witness, and there's your soul.

The personality – or ego – is very loud, very compelling, and quite reactive. The soul is quiet and still. The witness is your "gap" between stimulus and response, where you choose between your personality and your soul in any given moment.

The witness chooses what you are. Are you your ego-personality or are you your soul? It is your witness that chooses in every moment which you will appear to be. When you witness to your personality (or ego), you experience and express the effect of all of the social programming that you have been indoctrinated with since birth. When you witness to your soul, you experience and express what you came into this life for – and you experience the grandeur and beauty of genuine feeling.

It is wise to take time every day to be still and silent and allow your soul to whisper its desires in your consciousness. This "whisper" may take many forms. It is only the content that really matters. This content will be picked up pre-consciously and will help influence what information reaches your awareness throughout the day. Think of your preconscious as a gatekeeper of sensory information. Let your soul speak to this gatekeeper without interruption from your ego. If you are careful to do this often enough, you will notice a change in your environment. Situations will appear easier, more manageable. You will have a clearer idea of what it is you are going after. You will be more courageous in achieving what your soul really wants to achieve.

"I searched the Internet looking for answers ... I found none. I searched my heart ... and found many."

~ Garret LoPorto

There is a pattern to follow here:

Listen to your soul. Daydream, meditate, enjoy unstructured time ... Play & Pray.

Reinforce in your mind's eye the direction you are given. Visualize your soul's desire as already accomplished. Repeat this imagery until you are given something new from your soul.

Go about your business. Do what needs to be done. Clear away the rubble in your life – the unfinished actions, the "to do's", the promises, and the commitments.

When you run into trouble, move your mind back to that fluid, more dreamlike place and allow your unconscious mind to fill your awareness with encoded answers to your dilemma. Use your soul as your questioner, because your personality will ask poor questions and get confusing answers. But your soul knows the right questions to ask and your unconscious mind is ready to answer this call.

"When a soul wishes to experience something, she throws an image of the experience out before her and enters into her own image."

~ Meister Ekhart

Dreaming in a Sea of Answers

"I have discovered that it is of some use that when you lie in bed at night, and gaze into the darkness, to repeat in your mind the things you have been studying. Not only does it help the understanding, but also the memory."

~ Leonardo DaVinci

"An eminent New York professor related an illustrative story. He had been searching for a particular chemical formula for some time, but without success. One night, while he was sleeping, he had a dream in which the formula was worked out and displayed before him. He woke up, and in the darkness he excitedly wrote it down on a piece of tissue, the only thing he could find. But the next morning he could not read his own scribbling. Every night thereafter, upon going to bed, he would concentrate his hopes on dreaming that dream again. Fortunately, after some nights he did, and he then wrote the formula down for good. It was the formula he had sought and for which he received the Nobel Prize."[16]

DaVinci Children – Lost in the Dream

DaVinci types tend more towards Theta brainwave states – meaning they are often half dreaming. This is particularly obvious with DaVinci children. When you say something to them, it often doesn't register. When they don't want to comply with what you are saying they block you out of their private dream experience. So it's like your child is sleep-walking, sleep-running, sleep-climbing, sleep-living!

You can't shake them; and that often won't rouse them from their waking dream anyway. They are determined to live out whatever waking dream they are having, and they will stubbornly cling to exactly what it is they've set out to experience in this dream. Any sensory input that conflicts with their intended dream will be blocked out.

People operating from this dreamy state seem horribly self-absorbed and selfish – like they think no one else exists or matters – and this may not be far from the truth, because in the dream-state, people are dream figures trying to inflict their will on the dreamer. The dreamer just wants to have his dream; so he will banish people from his realm of perception if they aren't playing to his script. He will also distort people in his mind so that they appear to be playing to his script, even when they are not. (Also, because this is a form of using people, it creates guilt within the dreamer).

This dreamy refusal to acknowledge or respect any boundaries, directions, requests, or pleading from a parent can so frustrate and anger that parent, that they may become openly hostile toward the child. "Wake UP!! – YOU insolent maniac! Why won't you listen to me?!" they may cry to their child. Unfortunately all this does is introduce darkness into their dream – or temporarily shake them up enough to wake them for that moment, but at the expense of really hurting and upsetting them.

These DaVinci children tend to make much noise – as if it's an attempt to wake themselves up. What appears to be a large part of the motivation for being in a half-sleep is an avoidance of the pain and despair of feeling rejected, ignored and alone. DaVincis have an ultra high need for intimacy and soulful connection – and when they don't find that in their outside world they seek it within from their dreams. This is the root of the pseudo-narcissistic tendencies of DaVinci types.

The Struggle to Wake Up

All of this is not only true for DaVinci children. It is true for adults too, but for a somewhat mature ego, the dreaminess is considered a form of narcissism.

What makes all this dreaminess quite valuable is that these DaVinci types are channeling the intelligence of their profound and powerful unconscious mind through their day-dreaming activity. Through this half-dreaming activity these DaVincis will be bringing unconscious truths out into the open. They will be leading the way to greater truth and discovery, albeit often at the expense and comfort of the people close to them.

"GET OUT OF YOUR FOG – AND JOIN THE HUMAN RACE!!!" many close friends and relatives want to scream to this individual.

When you are not happy with your situation, you either engage (fight) or you go half-asleep (flight). Your half-asleep state can become the instigation of your disorder if you do not manage your states appropriately. Half asleep is a great way to discover transcendent solutions to impossible problems, but it's also a pathetic way to avoid the pain of your life. Theta brainwaves are what dominate your dreamy state, but that must be balanced with Alpha brainwaves, which make you come alive physically and help you feel wide awake. Alpha brainwaves are encouraged through physical encounters and exercise. Alpha brainwaves are also amplified in natural daylight while communing with nature. Running around in a grassy field is a great way to wake up and increase your Alpha brainwaves. Maybe that's why field sports are so popular.

When you are engaged, you become intimately aware of all the conflict in your life and that is quite upsetting. Take heart. Have courage. Your only way out is through awakening; not slipping into the oblivion of sleep.

I know it's difficult to wake up to all the chaos of life at times, but remember, "This too shall pass." Beyond that initial horror of waking awareness is the energy and confidence to keep going, because you will start seeing a way out of your scary predicament – and beyond that is the thrill of victory.

"Take the first step in faith. You don't have to see the whole staircase, just take the first step."

~ Dr. Martin Luther King Jr.

Being Brilliant & Awake

In order to be brilliant, you first need to wake up. Anyone who's gotten out of bed on a cold and early morning knows how much courage that can take.

Bono – lead singer for U2 – learned to wake himself up so he could communicate the songs he heard in his mind more powerfully to the outside world. He would jump up and down, jog around, get his blood pumping and break into a sweat before he sang his spontaneous stream-of-consciousness lyrics. Out of that came great songs like "In the name of Love" and "Bad" with its telling line "I'm wide awake!"

Be Kind to the Dreamer

Ever wonder who chooses the contents of your dreams?

Is it you? Is it some mysterious other-intelligence? Or is it just random?

Any good student of Freud's would say that dreams are made from our unconscious mind. They are a summation of our secret thoughts, wishes, fears and guilt. Dreams may feel like they have a reality outside of our own thinking, but they do not.

I watched the movie Vanilla Sky the other night. I love how it shows the role guilt plays in our dreams. Guilt can turn happy dreams into nightmares. Guilt can rob us of our greatest joys and replace them with self-punishment. In our dreams guilt can take the form of stalkers chasing us.

If life is but a dream, then guilt is what messes up our life. We cannot have a happy life if pangs of guilt hold our joys in check. We must first dissolve our guilt before our powerful unconscious mind will see us as deserving of happy dreams of love and gratitude.

Now it is clear why so many saints and enlightened ones have devoted their lives to service. It is a simple way to absolve oneself of guilt. It gives the dreaming mind reason to be kind to the dreamer.

Share What You Love
& the Money *Will* Follow

I always found, "Do what you love and the money will follow" to be too pat – too Pollyanna – too impractical. It seems to count on some benevolent Force in the Universe to come to the rescue and reward you for impractical courage.

The other detractor to that saying is the example of all the "starving artists" out there. They're doing what they love, hoping the money will follow, but it's not. Or maybe it is, but it might not get there until after they're dead.

The statement, "Do what you love and the money will follow" trusts in the power of love, which I agree with, but it does not seem to take into account the principles of money, commerce, transactions and wealth.

My friend, Martin Sussman, once said to me, "the amount of wealth a piece of currency produces is based on how much it is circulated. If you take one $20 bill and stuff it under your mattress, and you take another $20 bill and pay a masseuse for a massage, and she then uses that $20 to buy a dress, and the store owner then uses that money to buy lunch and the restaurant owner uses that money to buy the groceries and pay the cook and the cook uses that money to pay his rent, and the grocer uses that money to pay the farmers; that $20 bill – starting with your original transaction – has produced an accumulation of $80 of services and wealth through its circulation.

So it is with money that the more it is shared the more overall wealth it produces.

That being the case that old awkward cliché, "Do what you love and the money will follow" might be more helpful and true if it were to be "*Share* what you love and the money will follow."

It is through the *sharing* of what you love that value is brought into the world – the *doing* is only a fraction of the process.

Think of a guy who loves watching hockey. If he just sits around watching hockey, because he is doing what he loves, chances are he won't be making much money.

However, if he shares the love of watching hockey, by helping others to see the games too, say by being a hockey sportscaster, then he is actually *sharing* what he loves and it is easy to see how money will follow.

Another example is if you are a salesman who sells cars, but you love boating. You might not want to give up your sales career, buy a boat and go broke boating – you might want to become a boat salesman instead. That way you are sharing what you love – boating – not going broke trying to simply do what you love.

Sharing involves having a genuine encounter with others. Doing can be done in isolation. Do you see the difference? Do you see how to just "do what you love" can encourage selfishness and escapism, while having the courage to "share what you love" engenders greater awareness and selfless service to others?

Which approach do you think "the money will follow"?

"But how does this apply to one's art?" a fellow DaVinci once asked.

To give you some back-story, the particular artist who asked this question loves peoples' eyes. She is captivated by the soul that she sees through their eyes and this makes her want to draw their portrait.

I responded, "It can be your mission to share what you love through your art. Share the beauty that you see in peoples' eyes. Powerfully amplify the soul you see in those eyes, so that everyone, who looks at your portraits, is taken with the soul their eyes convey."

Your opportunity as an artist is to create what you love to behold. For through that creation you are making more of what you love and sharing it with the world.

Surfing Your Unconscious Mind

DaVincis are Adventurers

"Crisis is a terrible thing to waste."

The unconscious mind is an uncertain place. It is tumultuous. Like a great ocean, it can carelessly toss you around without any regard for your tiny consciousness.

Those who live on the edge of the unconscious are a rare breed. These are the ones who can stare into the abyss and feel more alive for it. They are content with uncertainty. They trust the one thing that strikes fear in most people's hearts – change. They hope for that quality of living called adventure. They are the DaVinci.

The unconscious mind is full of adventure, because as soon as it uproots your consciousness from control of the ego, it takes you on a wild ride through all the material that your conscious mind has been unwilling to see.

To live in a primarily Beta brainwave state is to live in a down-to-earth landlocked state. All of your experiences will tend toward the mundane – your experience is dry and concrete. This is a great state in which to do your taxes, accounting, pay the bills, and deal with the mundane aspects of physical existence. In these states you will likely be attentive, detail oriented, methodical and bored.

To embrace a primarily Alpha-Theta brainwave state is quite another experience. To live in Alpha-Theta brainwave states is to live on the edge of perpetual adventure – to be constantly charting new frontiers, exploring new territory, pushing the envelope, and diving in to the juice of life. These brainwave states are highly creative, completely outlandish (no pun intended), inexplicably deep and profound. Every moment, every motion, every detail is another piece of evidence for a divine answer being scrawled across the sky of your consciousness.

The old adage "Have your head in the clouds and your feet on the ground," is good guidance for how to live on the cusp of Alpha and Theta brainwave dominance. Theta is the receptive feminine intuitive region of thought, the proverbial "head in the clouds." Alpha is the projective masculine "gut" level of thought, it is the proverbial "feet on the ground." Alpha is what gives your Theta inspiration traction in your physical life.

When you are living from the Alpha region of your mind, you are grounded and externally aware. You have both feet planted firmly on the ground. If you feel like you may be too spacey, dreamy, or disconnected from your outer reality, then you need more Alpha. One way to increase your Alpha state is to walk barefoot on the grass. You are literally planting your feet on solid ground this way. It may sound hokey or overly symbolic, but it really works.

When you are living out of the Theta region of thought, even numbers aren't just dry data anymore; they are living symbols of a divine mystery. The symbolism that saturates every moment of consciousness is beckoning you to arrive at new awarenesses of the potential your situation offers you.

Nothing is ordinary in these states – it is all transcendent and sublime. This is not a good place to do your taxes from – far too much creativity lives here (and the IRS has been known to do its best to squash creativity.) ... but here is an oasis to discover solutions to the deeper mysteries of your life, this is *the place* to be.

Levels of Consciousness

Sigmund Freud taught that there are levels of consciousness. Each level has its own special properties and relationship with our overall life experience:

Conscious (tiny): the conscious mind only holds what you are immediately aware of. You can talk about your conscious experience, you can manipulate the items in your conscious mind and you can think about them in a logical way.

Pre-conscious (small): the pre-conscious (or subconscious) mind makes up your ordinary memory and is like a gate-keeper of what is allowed into your consciousness. So although you aren't necessarily aware of what's going on in your pre-conscious mind, you can readily access it.

Unconscious (huge): Freud taught that this part of the mind is not directly accessible to conscious awareness. In part, he saw it as a dumping ground for urges, feelings and ideas that are rejected by your conscious mind – most often they are associated with pain, and conflict. According to Freud, when feelings and thoughts are rejected or denied by the conscious mind they do not just go away. They sit in your unconscious exerting influence on your body, actions, dreams and conscious awareness. This is where most of the work of the Id and Superego take place.

Material passes back and forth easily between the conscious and the preconscious. Material from these two areas can also slip into the unconscious.

Iceberg Metaphor
for the Levels of the Mind:

"Water is the driving force of all nature."

~ Leonardo da Vinci

The unconscious mind is often represented by water. A model that Sigmund Freud and Carl Jung use to describe the levels of the mind is an iceberg. The part of the iceberg that is above the surface of the water is your conscious mind. Consciousness is the part of your mind you know directly. It is where you are self-aware of your thoughts, feelings, senses and intuitions. It is through conscious activity that you see yourself as an individual. It's the part of your mind that contains information in your immediate awareness.

Beneath the lowest level of your consciousness, there is a waterline (to stay with this iceberg metaphor), beneath this waterline is the rest of the iceberg – the preconscious (or subconscious) and the unconscious.

What Freud calls the unconscious, is what Jung calls the "personal unconscious." Here you will find thoughts, feelings, urges, memories and impulses that are rejected by your consciousness. Experiences that do not reach consciousness, experiences that are not congruent with who you think you are, and things that have become "repressed" make up the material beneath the level of consciousness.

Only 10% of an iceberg is truly visible (conscious) while the other 90% is submerged beneath the water (below consciousness is preconscious and unconscious).

The Preconscious could be 10% to 15% while the Unconscious is overwhelmingly huge and could be anywhere from 80%-97% of your mind's capacity.

Although not directly accessible, material in your personal unconscious has gotten there sometime during your lifetime. For example, the words you choose to describe yourself, why you pick a particular partner or your career may be choices you reached consciously. But it is more likely that these choices have been influenced by personal unconscious material like your parents' preferences, formative childhood experiences, and even television programming you may have seen. You do not think about these influences consciously when you make your decisions, but unconsciously your mind bursts forth with this unconscious programming under the veil of situational choices.

Depth psychologists hold that most of your decisions are determined by unconscious factors.[17]

Unconscious Body Signals

Your unconscious mind runs most of your body functions. It runs your digestive system, your immune system, etcetera, and your unconscious mind has the capacity to use your body as a communication channel to reach your conscious awareness. For many the most they perceive is that they are suddenly sick or have heartburn, a nervous stomach, a headache, sweaty palms or any myriad of physical ailments that are chalked up to chance. But what if your unconscious mind is trying to tell you something with increasing intensity, by generating these ailments? This question is exactly what got Sigmund Freud the medical doctor to become the father of modern psychology and psychoanalysis.

Freud had many patients who had physical symptoms and maladies with no underlying physical cause. He then noticed that they had dreams that reflected psychological causes for these symptoms. He later said "Dreams are the royal road to the unconscious." But originally what tipped Freud off that there was even such a thing as the unconscious mind was patients with physical symptoms without physical causes.

The son of George Soros (the great billionaire currencies investor) describes how his father recognizes his back pain as a messenger communicating to him from the deep wisdom of his unconscious mind, which George Soros uses to help him select his investments (and surf his unconscious):

> *"My father will sit down and give you theories to explain why he does this or that. But I remember seeing this as a kid and thinking, 'At least half of this is bull.' I mean, you know the reason he changes his position in the market or whatever is because his back starts killing him.*
> *He literally goes into a spasm, and it's his early warning sign."*
>
> ~ Son of George Soros,
> billionaire currencies investor

As I've become more inwardly honest, I've developed awareness of subtle unconscious clues sent to me through my body. My throat will tighten when I am speaking wrongly, lying or misleading myself and others with what I am saying. I take this to mean, "Whoa! Off course" from my deeper wisdom. If I'm not too firmly entrenched in my ego at the moment, I will quickly change the subject or the content of what I am saying in order to re-align with the highest purpose of the moment.

I also have these twitches all throughout my body - very subtle, imperceptible to other people, small strands of muscle somewhere in my body will unexpectedly twitch in order to deliver me a message. If the twitch is on my left side I have come to understand this means 'no' or 'false' to whatever thought was passing through my mind in that instant. If the twitch is somewhere on the right-hand side of my body, it is a sign of affirmation of whatever I was thinking at that moment. This is basic self intelligence.

Then I can often subconsciously escalate this information for confirmation to my highest wisdom and I will get a light sensation and a buzz on the top right of my skull as if I were being touched there tenderly - then I know a higher intelligence has given approval to my conscious thought at that moment. This very phenomenon has led the writing of this, which has met with some gentle editing from what I experience as a higher source.

Imagination

> *"I believe that imagination is stronger than*
> *knowledge - myth is more potent than history*
> *- dreams are more powerful than facts*
> *- hope always triumphs over experience*
> *- laughter is the cure for grief*
> *- love is stronger than death"*

~ Robert Fulghum

Your unconscious mind is holistic, meaning it thinks in wholes. So whenever you are stuck in the middle of something, your unconscious mind tends to have the completion of that something waiting for you. It's like when you sing the melody or knock the rhythm to the famous "Shave and a hair cut ... Two bits!" If you were to stop before singing the last two notes, your unconscious mind would leap in to complete it for you. Such is the way all your problems can be solved, simply **START** the melody and your unconscious mind will work day and night to complete your situation. That is why affirmations and visualizations work so well. That is why just diving in and beginning something has so much more power than waiting for 'the right time'. Once you begin it, once you are committed to seeing an action through, your unconscious mind rushes to your aid to help you complete it.

It is also important to be aware that besides your unconscious mind you must have a good guidance system. If you allow your ego to be your guide you will merely manifest ever larger portraits of your own ego. All of your problems will be multiplied in the ever increasing image of your ego. If you choose to invite the "still small voice" of God for highest good (also known as "compassion" or the Holy Spirit), this Spirit will guide your unconscious mind to provide you with answers that manifest grace instead of bigger problems.

Think of your unconscious mind as a neutral genie of a magic lamp that gives you free wishes. This genie will answer your questions and grant your wishes no matter how troublesome this may be to you. So it is you who must be careful what you ask for, because any error in your request can have far-reaching and disastrous results. There is an old curse that goes "May you get what you want!"

Your ego can only ask questions based on your social conditioning. So these questions will just be regurgitations of what your parents and your culture have programmed you to ask. These kinds of questions, when asked, rarely have a truly positive outcome.

On the other hand, your soul came into this life with questions – good questions – that deep down you truly long to hear the answers to. It is rediscovering what these questions are that will bring you joy.

Always use God, Compassion, Jesus Christ, the Holy Spirit or another ambassador of Absolute Goodness to guide you in what questions you ask your unconscious mind. Then you are using your power wisely.

"When human power becomes so great and original that we can account for it only as a kind of divine imagination, we call it genius"

~ William Crashaw

Elegance

"Simplicity is the ultimate sophistication."

~ Leonardo da Vinci

Beauty and elegance are the qualities of inspiration. The unconscious mind will often offer beautiful and elegant solutions to your problems – and it is precisely their beauty and elegance that immediately makes us aware of this particular thought or vision's value.

This is why physicists and mathematicians are concerned with the elegance of a formula or theory. It is elegance that signals this answer is not a complicated and contrived concoction of the ego. This answer has the simplicity, beauty and grace of truth.

The unconscious mind seeks to make the conscious mind whole. The unconscious mind restores balance, completes the incomplete and finishes the song in a graceful twist. Your vastly powerful unconscious mind knows how it can impress your consciousness with beauty and so it uses wholeness, elegance and beauty as a form to signal "pay attention to this."

Another impressive quality of most unconscious insights is the perfect fit. Like that piece that fits perfectly in the dizzying jigsaw puzzle, the solutions offered by your unconscious mind can solve every nuance of your situation so precisely with such quintessential perfection that it feels as if God had designed your entire life in preparation for unveiling this breathtaking solution.

Your experience of "I had no idea. ... I had no idea! How could I have missed this all that time?" This experience could be called a revelation.

Or if you want to see it more objectively, these dawns of unconscious genius awaken you to the realization that the universe shines forth in simple and perfect radiance, and continues to do so, whether you're ever aware of it or not.

> *"Human subtlety will never devise an invention more beautiful, more simple or more direct than does nature because in her inventions nothing is lacking, and nothing is superfluous."*
>
> ~ Leonardo da Vinci

Beauty is Truth

How could anything be wrong in a moment of perfect beauty? That's how answers are given to us, our perception is merely shifted to see the perfect beauty of a particular situation. If you thought there was a problem before you saw the beauty of the moment – in witnessing that perfect beauty – the solution becomes clear, because the solution is part of that beauty.

What we once saw as ugliness was merely half the picture. When we don't see the beauty of a situation – we are only seeing half of the picture. Once we see the whole picture, we notice the sublime beauty of how every answer is part of the question. It is often the poor question that draws a line between itself and the answer we are looking for. Once we see the beauty of our situation, we begin to ask better questions and the answers are clear. We realize then that every ugly "problem" is actually a beautiful situation, that through too limited a view, we have misunderstood.

Forgiveness is another way of describing this ultimate problem solving process. Forgiveness sees how one is truly perfect and in witnessing that perfection in all its beauty, the ugliness is dissolved in the context of that sublime beauty.

"There are no problems – only solutions."

~ John Lennon

The Whole Disaster

In our repressed and mechanized society, the "messiness" of irrational unconscious impulses is seen as a grave threat. These impulses betray the controlled social norms. They force us to look at what is really happening to our souls beneath the cool disinterest we charade around in.

A great spiritual teacher once taught that the first step towards enlightenment is to admit that "your life is in a mess." So it is what DaVincis naturally do. They expose the mess, which is just below the surface of everyone's social veneer.

The bourgeoisie maintain their place in society by keeping the status quo. The bourgeoisie is the part of the middle class that spends most of their time maintaining and reinforcing the social norms of their community, mostly out of fear of losing social status. They don't like having the proverbial boat rocked; because if their community shifts in any way, chances are their place in it will collapse. It is easy to see why the Normal type behaves this way, because the Normal type is far less able to adapt to change than the DaVinci type.

During times of change DaVinci types thrive, because of their adaptability, ingenuity and novelty seeking behavior. On the other hand, during periods of monotony the Normal type thrives because of the comfort they find in a steady adherence to societal, cultural and social rules, plus the enjoyment they find in performing the same repetitive duties, day in and day out.

Since 90% of the world population is the Normal type, you can see why so much of our society revolves around abiding by rules and regulations. If you take a close look at our school systems, you'll note that, (more than even teaching reading, writing and arithmetic), they indoctrinate students into a culture of rules. Boundaries are important to be aware of, but when rules are worshipped over common sense or compassion, then that is when the DaVincis in the ranks tend to take matters into their own hands.

Most Normal types on some level recognize that they are only contributing to their organization as a "cog in the wheel," not as a leader or free thinker. They have spent the better part of their lives training to become really good at playing their part as this "cog in the wheel," and that is where they get their pride from. If that "wheel" changes, chances are that their particular place as a cog in that wheel will be outmoded.

While DaVinci types would celebrate the opportunity to do something new and different, this terrifies the Normal type. The Normal type's fear is that they will be unable (or unwilling) to adapt and they will be abandoned by their organization as useless. So, these Normal types will do everything in their power to keep things as they are.

As long as everything appears fine, the bourgeoisie gets to keep their comfortable lot in society. They are the last who would admit there is a mess right below the surface of things. The bourgeoisie maintain their place in society by subduing insurgence, shaming the unexpected, and snuffing the spirit of DaVinci types. Anyone not following the "rules" of society is swiftly put down by the bourgeoisie.

A commonly given reason for their approach to life is "because it's always been done that way." This kind of thinking drives DaVincis nuts. DaVincis are always finding new flaws to fix and new ways of doing things, and this threatens the Normal types around them. If the Normal type has some kind of authority over the DaVinci type, that's when rebellion is likely to occur.

A collaborator in this bourgeois conspiracy is the severe neurotic DaVinci type. The severe neurotic is wounded from their early experiences of having their own spontaneity and innovativeness punished out of them. They now feel the fear of that punishment being repeated whenever anyone within their sphere of influence exercises that same kind of spontaneous freedom. They also have internalized that punishment so that whenever they themselves have a spontaneous impulse, they sublimate it through an inner form of torture. So now, instead of encouraging freedom in their fellow DaVinci types as their true DaVinci nature would suggest, they have a reaction response to spontaneous freedom that reminds them of all the punishment they once endured. That's when they tend to get a sadistic charge out of forcefully suppressing and punishing these other DaVincis.

So, not all of the bourgeois oppressors are Normal types. Some of the worst of them are wounded neurotic DaVinci types who can't stand to see others enjoying the freedom they never got to.

Remember, the power of the DaVincis is our deep connection with the unconscious and our ability to freely and spontaneously reveal deep truths. This is threatening to the Normal type because of its disruptiveness. The messy truth that erupts from the depths of the unconscious mind simply doesn't fit nicely in the established "order" of a rules based society.

This spontaneous freedom is threatening to the severely neurotic DaVinci types because these revelations are often messy and remind them of wounds they have endured for similar behavior.

To further tip the odds in the favor of suppression of deep and genuine emotion, technology now helps defend our society's increasingly lifeless status quo. You may note that whenever there is a chance encounter with a deep and genuine truth – or whenever there is an intimate moment welling from our depths – there is always a cell phone to save us from that beautiful experience.

*"That's the beauty of Television. Whenever there
is something really important happening on TV ...
you can always turn the channel."*

~ Bono

Developing Your
Gift for Problem Solving

It has been said that DaVinci types have, on average, 20% higher IQs than the rest of the population. This is due largely to the amazing problem solving capacity of people with DaVinci wired brains.

Most IQ tests are designed to prefer lateral thinking ability over linear thinking because it is a greater sign of high intelligence. Albert Einstein was primarily a lateral thinker, as was Thomas Edison, Benjamin Franklin, and Leonardo da Vinci.

Lateral thinking is a problem-solving approach where you attempt many different angles in order to find a solution. You think "outside the box" and you discover many new ways of framing problems rather than staying stuck.

People who are highly capable lateral thinkers are great solution finders; inventors, entrepreneurs, pioneers, explorers and artists. Their temperaments tend to be creative, energetic, impulsive and "distractible" because those are the qualities that facilitate great lateral thinking ability. Leonardo da Vinci epitomized this kind of temperament.

DaVincis excel at lateral thinking ability. Lateral thinking is most effective in certain environments - generally situations where there is little or no established procedure for success - situations where the solution must be discovered as opposed to merely regurgitated.

Most entrepreneurs, inventors and pioneers find themselves in circumstances where strong lateral problem solving ability is a greater asset than any formula one might have memorized. Lateral thinking is creative and difficult to teach anyone who doesn't already have a penchant for it. It is the opposite of linear thinking, which is the kind of thinking encouraged and graded for in most public school systems.

"If you are a genius, boredom can be dangerous."

~ Sherlock Holmes on PBS

MENSA riddles can be used to further develop and hone this gift. MENSA riddles offer the following therapeutic benefits to DaVincis:

1) Difficult, sometimes baffling, genius caliber MENSA riddles are often compelling enough to capture the attention of DaVinci types and evoke their hyper-focus.

2) Good MENSA riddles have satisfying and elegant solutions, which are in and of themselves reward enough for the mental effort required to crack them.

3) MENSA riddles are a great mental workout – similar in effect to physical exercise – because they calm and focus the DaVinci mind by releasing pent up energy.

4) MENSA riddles build self-esteem with each subsequent victory and show the neurotic DaVinci how brilliant they really are.

5) The mental effort required to do MENSA riddles effectively exercises your DaVinci mind, making you smarter and smarter. (I have seen my problem-solving ability boosted dramatically simply by doing a handful of MENSA riddles every day for just a few weeks.)

6) The solution finding ability that doing MENSA riddles develops in your mind makes solving other day-to-day life problems surprisingly easier.

If you would like to try a couple great MENSA riddles refer to Appendix A at the end of this book.

The Socratic Method

"I never teach my pupils; I only attempt to provide the conditions in which they can learn."

~ Albert Einstein

The Socratic Method is a way of educating yourself by the original meaning of the word "educate." The Latin meaning of educate is "to draw out."

Socrates found the best way to cultivate wisdom in his students was not by telling them things – which is called didactic instruction – but to have them tell him things, which is now called Socratic instruction.

Didactic instruction is when the lecturer imposes information on students. So the didactic method basically means the student sits and consumes information, and is expected to learn by that process.

Socrates strongly believed that the didactic process did not cultivate any real wisdom. It, at best, encouraged students to be good regurgitators of information. In a didactic situation, students often memorize information and repeat "facts," without fully comprehending what it was that they were repeating.

Since Socrates was a teacher of great depth and of quite subtle philosophy, he needed a way to teach his students in a much more thorough, impactful way. What he discovered was that the Socratic Method – which is basically to ask good leading questions of his students – would draw out of them powerful new realizations through this questioning process.

Basically, in the Socratic Method, it is the students that are coming up with the information. It is the teacher that is supplying inspiration for coming up with that information. So good questions, good speaking assignments if you will, allow students to start speaking and start coming out with surprising new realizations.

This is all based on the principle that the truth is inside of you, and everything you need to know you already know, you just might need help navigating and accessing that knowledge.

How can you practice the Socratic Method?

You can practice the Socratic Method by finding a friend or hiring someone who will genuinely listen to you with the real intent to hear your deepest wisdom speak. You will be amazed what happens when one person listens to another with the expectation of hearing something powerful and profound.

Once you have a great listener to help you, speak on whatever subject you are most interested in learning about. The other thing is if you already feel like you have somewhat of a grasp on the subject, you can speak about that and become more masterful of that.

What is interesting about the Socratic Method is that it is used all the time but by the people who espouse to be "teaching" – but they are really the learners because they are the ones being educated. It turns out that we as a culture have teaching and learning reversed!

All of those "thought leaders," who are paid to lecture on particular subjects are often the ones who are learning the most from their own lecture, because they have a captive audience that is performing the Socratic Method for them.

So, find your audience! Whether you need to start with a friend or ask someone to help – just start speaking. Start "talking out" all of your issues. What you will discover is as you continue to speak, if you have a good listener who is truly listening for your deepest wisdom to speak, is that there is actually some sort of deeper connection that makes you smarter. Just by being listened to this way, you are actually smarter!

You can use the Socratic Method to overcome your neurotic tendencies and exercise your will, by doing public presentations.

You can help yourself discover the ability to articulate genius solutions by combining the Socratic Method and Image-Streaming process described in this book.

The Birth of Unconscious Genius

Deep unconscious insights into profound awareness of your situation will sometimes break into your consciousness. These insights are usually a statement *against* what you have been trying to think consciously and rationally. If you have a perception, position, or belief you hold dear, chances are you are working hard trying to prove it and your consciousness is vigilant against information and arguments that might disprove it.

Your unconscious mind – if given the chance – will break through in direct opposition to any inaccurate conscious beliefs to which you are clinging too tightly.

Carl Jung often said there is a polarity between the unconscious and conscious. There is push and pull between these two aspects of your mind.

Your conscious mind keeps trying to frame the wild tides of your unconscious mind. By framing this vast ocean of thought your conscious mind for a moment feels in control, safe and stable. On the other hand, your unconscious mind washes up against your arid little desert islands of conscious "control" with the unpredictable but living tides of truth. The truth is that there is no "control," there just *is*. The little desert islands of control are an illusion in your consciousness that make you feel distinct. But your unconscious mind is not separate from you – it *is* you.

The unconscious mind recognizes the duality and treachery of logic without soul, of ego illusions of control, of jealous islands of individualism held against oceans of love and mercy. The unconscious mind can knock down the ego's ivory towers, because the unconscious mind is in control of 90% of what you do. So it is that any untrue conviction you hold too dear, any unhelpful belief you identify with too strongly, can be overruled by your unconscious mind.

If there is any self-deception in your stance – when you least expect it – your unconscious mind will burst forth, toppling your self-deceptions down along with every little thing those delusions have propped up in your life.

You Are Not Just Your *Conscious* Mind

You are not your conscious mind – you only wish you were, because you wish you had control. But you don't because your unconscious mind is so much more powerful in influencing the course of your life – much more than you even realize.

You wish you had control because you believe you are responsible for creating yourself – that you are a "self-made man" – but you are not.

Your conscious mind has no real control. It only has moments of volition. The course your life takes will either be one of struggle or ease, but either way you are going to end up in the same place eventually. (Mind you, that "place" here is not necessarily somewhere physical, or situational, but that place *is* honesty.) Because, eventually, no matter how hard you struggle against it – even if it's with your last breath – you will encounter the truth of your being and you will either be amazed or ashamed. You get to choose.

There is a struggle within you, between what you think you believe – the perspectives you cherish and identify with – and a new truer awareness struggling to be born. Before this new awareness is fully born, there is the pain of labor, the anxiety of being lost, the guilt of killing your old views – of killing who you were in order to be born into the awareness of who you truly are.

Breakthrough anxiety

"Every great idea starts out as blasphemy."

~ Bertrand Russell

Whenever a new perspective is born, it signals the demise of its predecessors. Whenever a true breakthrough in thought occurs it rattles a lot of cages, it destroys what many hold dear, it forces everyone to face the discomfort of being wrong, and forces them into change. The more wide-sweeping the impact of your breakthroughs the more anxiety and guilt you are likely to feel during the birthing of that creation.

"Genius is always allowed some leeway, once the
hammer has been pried from its hands and the
blood has been cleaned up"

~ Terry Pratchett

The anxiety is also due to the tremors you feel in the shaking of your self-world relationship. Your sense of identity is threatened. Your world is not as you thought it was before. You are disoriented in the vastness of the new paradigm you have conceived. Your old foundations are found faulty, weak and wanting and you must now uproot to the new and unknown.

Since your sense of self and your sense of your world are intimately intertwined, the rattling of your sense of your world implicitly rattles you. If the world is no longer what you thought before, then with regards to your relationship with your world, you are no longer what you thought you were.

An Extreme Example

I had a dream last night that I was a soldier in a war – only in this war there were strange customs. We met as a group of six soldiers with a group of six enemy soldiers and we were to play some sick game of strategy, skill and marksmanship that would leave most of us dead and the few left living were the victors.

I was freaked out. I shot the first enemy general to move in this "game." He was "full of honor" so, even after being lethally shot by me, he retraced his steps and attempted to perform his "move" cleanly without any illegal interruptions. I just kept shooting at him until he was dead. I was that freaked out.

Then I began shooting other members of the enemy team that I thought might retaliate for my misdeed. As the dream went on, I discovered to my horror that I hadn't understood the context of what was happening – we had called a truce without my realizing it – and I was not a hero, but a villain. This definitely shook my perception of my world and thus shook my perception of me.

The Authentic Encounter

On a more peaceful note, an authentic emotional encounter with someone will always change, to some degree, your self-world relationship – and to what degree you cannot know until the encounter has passed. So with every surrendering to an authentic encounter you are letting go of all you hold dear, possibly to never return to that sentiment.

This is a huge risk as far as our egos are concerned. Our ego's power and sense of control is based on attachment to our view of the world, and a single authentic encounter can uproot all of that attachment leaving us without any ego foundation with which to comprehend our world and manipulate it to our benefit.

The anxiety we feel stems from the apprehension of this momentary rootlessness, this dizzying and disorienting falling away from our previous strongholds on our world view. This is the anxiety of the 'nothingness' prescribed by Buddhist doctrine.

But finally at the culmination of this great birthing ordeal you will experience unspeakable joy – for you have found yourself new and reborn, fresh and new, with greater innocence and vitality at your command. You have arrived with the mythological "elixir" described in Joseph Campbell's famous Hero's Journey. The world may someday thank you for that.

The DaVinci are distinguished from the Normal type in their capacity to accept and live more fully in this ambiguity. Being adventurers and risk-takers, the thrill of the unknown – even if it is of the self – is worth the adventure.

Dreaming, Prayer & Image Streaming

This is where you gain direction. Make sure you are asking the right source for your imagery. When you dream pray and image stream, you are given guidance and clues on where to go, what to focus on, and how to get there (in one piece).

Dreaming

> *"Why does the eye see a thing more clearly in dreams than the imagination when awake?"*
>
> ~ Leonardo da Vinci

Remember your dreams. They are a key to your discovery process. They contain clues about everything you have been unwilling to see, they expose all of your hidden agendas – even the ones you hide from yourself.

Thomas Edison always took a cat nap in order to come up with solutions to his toughest problems. Right as he would begin to drift off into dreaming an insight would flash across his mind showing him what he was looking for.

Keep a journal or tape-recorder handy by your bed. While you are still in the foggy aftermath of a dream, you can still easily remember the contents of that dream because your mind is still in close resonance with that frequency. Do what you can to write or record a message to your wakeful self that will communicate the spirit imagery and apparent messages of your dream, for you may not recall much when your brain returns to its denser beta brainwave state.

Tips for Better Dream Recall

Before falling asleep:

✓ Expect to remember your dreams

✓ Be ready to record your dreams

✓ Ask your higher self to guide you in your dreams

✓ Ask your unconscious mind to answer a particular question

Upon waking:

✓ When you wake in the morning, don't move. Relax and let your mind drift close to the dream.

✓ Try to stay in your bridge consciousness (the consciousness between dreaming and full wakefulness).

✓ Remember your dream backwards. Follow the sequence of your dream as far back as you can.

- ✓ Remember as much as you can in this bridge consciousness, because when you fully wake up anything you haven't gotten across the bridge will fall back into your unconscious.

- ✓ Review in your mind the whole sequence of your dream a few times while you are still in your bridge consciousness

- ✓ What associations do you feel with various aspects of your dream story and your life story while you are still in bridge consciousness?

- ✓ Now write it all down.

- ✓ Review your dream diary later in the day when you are fully alert and awake. You may be amazed at what you discover.

Interpreting Your Dreams

What did you learn?

If your dream tells a story, discovering the meaning may be as simple as seeing the moral of the story. What did you learn from your dream experience? If you could relive that experience what would you do differently? On some level you *wanted* to have this dream; so what secret wish does it reveal?

Use Active Imagination

Mentally evoke a character from your dream and ask it questions. Imagine your dream character answering you. Just let this process flow naturally, without forcing any responses from your dream character and you may discover a great deal.

Recognizing Symbols & Archetypes

Brainstorm – using free association –all of the different symbolic associations with the different aspects of your dream.

Common Universal Symbols:

- ► House: the self

- ► Weather: what one is going through in life

- ► Water: the unconscious, the emotions, the source of life. Type of water and movement of water give clues about what is happening in the feelings and the unconscious. Dark murky water can be a warning that something bad is about to happen. Conversely, clear aqua blue water portents positive things in the future.

- ► Time of day: the time of one's life or one's state of being. (Dawn: youth, optimism; dusk: withdrawal, approaching death)

- ► People known to you: a particular quality of yourself

- ► Strangers: qualities of yourself that you do not own

- ► Animals: compulsive or habitual ways of thinking and acting.

- ► Death: change

- ► Black horse: refusal to exercise free will

- ► Vehicles: information about your physical body

- ► Shoes: your mental or spiritual foundation

- ► Clothing: one's outer expression

- ► Naked: you have opened up in your waking life or let the walls down. Represents a desire to communicate more deeply with others

- ► Flying: exercising free will powerfully

- ► Running away and finding your feet and legs are moving, but you are not moving forward: trying to do too many things at once and never seeming to get ahead.

▶ Moving at will: being decisive, goal-oriented

These universal meanings and generalized definitions are of minimal value in relation to self-understanding and personal growth.

Only through discovering one's own translations of symbols and images can the individual effect change or gain insight.

Symbols change meaning according to the context in which they appear and the personal experiences of the dreamer.

Personal symbols are formed in the unconscious and are tailored to reflect the person's life experience and emotion. The unconscious is able to create a symbol to illustrate a particular inner message.

Understanding personal symbols is one of the primary goals of dream work.

Listen to Your Dream's Soundtrack

My dreams often have some sort of song playing like a soundtrack in the background. Other times I may just wake up with a song playing in my head.

Either way if the song is something I've heard before and I can just keep the tune in mind long enough to recognize the name of the song, I can go download that track off the internet and listen to it.

Often when I am more awake the lyrics will reveal a hidden message from my unconscious.

When I am in a truly creative place the songs I hear in my dreams are originals – tunes I've never heard before – and I'll often try to steal them and record them myself.

Once I got a tune from a band playing it in my dream. It was a great little tune, so I remembered it and recorded it myself. As I was doing this I actually felt a twinge of guilt because it felt like I was stealing this song from the characters in my dream who wrote it. If I ever meet them again I will apologize.

Prayer

> *"Where the spirit does not work with the hand*
> *there is no art"*

> ~ Leonardo da Vinci

The Prayer I'm talking about here is the pursuit of answers to your life questions. Often people confuse this (or rather reduce this) to asking for things. The trouble with that is that you already have everything you could ask for. The whole of creation is already yours, it is only the beliefs in your mind that make that seem not so.

When my son John was just three my wife used to say as we would walk through a vast field, parking lot or store, "John, all of this is yours." And he believed it and he felt content. Native Americans had a similar belief – one that we all share everything and that there really is no such thing as personal property. This reframing of our world makes you free to want what you really want and not be distracted by artificial wants for things merely generated by ideas of scarcity.

Prayer offers you a way to leave the perspective of scarcity for a moment and commune at the level of God. When you are praying with God, you are no longer in want, for you are in 'have.'

> *"Seek ye first for the kingdom of heaven and all*
> *else will be added on to you"*

When you reach a state of true prayerfulness your mind will surrender its clinging to all the scarcity driven wants it was attached to. With this new emptiness and buoyancy God can pour into your mind the gifts of having – of having peace, of having courage, of having answers.

Prayers are answered the moment your heart feels them. Then it is just a matter of surrendering control of your mind to God long enough for him to *show* you the answers to your prayers. That's a bit different than God doing something to change the world in order to answer your prayers. Instead, God will often show you how the world is already perfect, and your prayers are already answered, if you can only have the right perspective.

Also recognize that prayer is best guided by God, so you may ask the first questions, but then it is good to let God show you more helpful questions to be answered.

The whole purpose of prayer is to allow God to realign your mind with His – to provide you with better questions to ask – to show you which direction to go.

> *"He who loves practice without theory is like the sailor who boards ship without a rudder and compass and never knows where he may cast."*
>
> ~ Leonardo da Vinci

Image Streaming

Image streaming is the act of daydreaming with the intention of having particular questions answered by your unconscious mind. Your unconscious mind is like an all knowing supercomputer with no one to direct it, save your consciousness or God's.

So image streaming is like tuning into your supercomputer's interface and utilizing its incredible power to answer any question you may have.

Now, mind you, the quality of the questions you ask will determine the quality of the answers you receive. It is best to have received good questions to ask through honest prayer, before proceeding to tap your unconscious for solutions.

Think of prayer as the riddle provider and image streaming as the solution provider. Your unconscious mind – especially the id – is like a great wild stallion, and the memory of God personified is the only adequate rider of this powerful stallion.

When you image stream all you need to do is ask a question, then close your eyes and describe into a recording device every image that crosses your mind. Then ask the same question again and repeat the process. Now finally ask your unconscious mind how these two solutions are the same and again watch the imagery that occurs and record it.

Now become fully awake again and reflect on what your recordings are telling you.

One way to make this process even purer is to come up with about fifty different questions and write them all down on little pieces of paper. Put them all into a hat and blindly pick one without reading it. Do your image streaming process with the intention of answering the unopened question you have picked. Think Johnny Carson's The Great Carnac. He's wearing a turban holding up sealed envelopes to his forehead and answering questions before he reads them.

Remember your unconscious mind is knowing and powerful indeed. *It* knows which question you picked, but now your conscious mind's preconceptions can't get in the way as covertly. You will more easily notice if you seem to have some preconception of what question is being asked and your mind keeps steering you to what you already believe the answer should be.

Clearing the Rats from Your Basement

*"The depth and strength of a human character are
defined by its moral reserves.
People reveal themselves completely only when
they are thrown out of the customary conditions of
their life, for only then do they have to fall back on
their reserves."*

~ Leonardo da Vinci

In the end, the reason social programming works is because it lets people disguise their unconscious guilt and aggression with a face of innocence.

Freud said "Civilization began the first time an angry person cast a word instead of a rock." So it is with social programming, we are taught to behave in a socially acceptable way – which means we deny what we are and become what is acceptable. We do not do what we are impelled by our souls to do, instead we do only what our social conditioning allows us.

This works well for the Normal type, because they are naturally much more repressed than the DaVinci type anyway. So simply molding their overall repression to mimic social and societal norms is quite easy and pleasant for the Normal type.

On the other hand, the DaVinci type has very little natural repression available to him. So there is often not enough of this natural repression available for him to cover all the social boundaries he is told to heed. His being is far too irrepressible to control this way. Just to fit in and avoid punishment most DaVinci do try – but they have to use vigilant conscious monitoring instead of being able to rely on the natural bed of repression Normal types enjoy. During their vigil of behavioral repression the DaVincis begin to feel strained and claustrophobic – like they are going to burst – until at last they finally do burst.

The DaVinci psyche is not designed for repression – it is designed for clearing. Clearing is the immediate release of unresolved unconscious issues through physical, verbal and emotional expression. This is a beautiful healing phenomenon, but it can be quite unseemly from the "cool" social perspective.

DaVincis are at their best when they are surfing the tide of their unconscious impulses and choosing the waves of impulses that originate from their souls. These unconscious impulses lead DaVincis to do wild and spontaneous things that are often sublimely perfect for the moment they happen in. The trouble is they are often not-at-all anticipated by cultural/social and societal norms. These actions are purely original and unexpected. Because of this they threaten to undermine the very fabric the Normal type has based his repressed existence on – and so these actions are often met with much disdain and shaming.

Also these actions – because they are often actions of clearing – reveal layers of collective unconscious guilt and hostility, which in the light of day can be healed. Because most are not comfortable being affronted with one's guilt and hostility, there is the strong temptation to "kill the messenger."

A DaVinci must often clear all his subconscious guilt and aggression first, before reaching the beauty of the divine impulses beneath. We call this uncomfortable period "Clearing the Rats from your Basement."

Based on C.S. Lewis's metaphor of "rats in the cellar," we can come to understand a primary difference between the DaVinci and the Normal type.

> "The excuse that immediately springs to mind, is that the provocation was so sudden or unexpected I was caught off my guard. I had not time to collect myself. Surely

what a man does when he is taken off guard is the best evidence for what sort of man he is. Surely what pops out, before the man has time to put on a disguise, is the truth.

If there are rats in the cellar you are most likely to see them if you go in very suddenly. But the suddenness does not create the rats. It only prevents them from hiding. In the same way, the suddenness of the provocation does not make me an ill tempered man. It only shows me what an ill tempered man I am.

Now that cellar is out of reach of my conscious will. I cannot, by direct moral effort, give myself new motives.

After the first few steps we realize that everything which really needs to be done in our souls can be done only by God."

~ C.S. Lewis

For the most part the Normal type has the door to his cellar tightly locked – meaning his consciousness is firmly closed, tightly repressing the vicissitudes of his unconscious mind. On the other hand the DaVinci type – being more open to conscious awareness of the unconscious desires and impulses – has left his door to the cellar ajar; and rats will escape every now and then.

The basement is a powerful place, and – once it is free of rats – it is a storehouse of amazing wealth that can supply one with an abundance of creative inspiration and brilliance. But while rats still lurk in this storehouse, one will be subject to inevitable disturbances by them. Since DaVincis can only hold the door to their cellars closed with great effort and conscious exertion – it is best to surrender to the task of clearing out the rats, instead of merely trying to hide them behind a flimsy door of behavioral repression.

Surrender to the task of clearing the rats out of your basement, for once you have accomplished this you will be rewarded with the boon of abundant energy, creativity and grace – you will be living as a 'total human;' from basement to attic; and you will be able to harness a power so great it has been the subject of every mythology since the dawn of man.

> *"Even the richest soil, if left uncultivated will*
> *produce the rankest weeds."*
>
> ~ Leonardo da Vinci

Refusing to clear the cellar condemns one to always being haunted by their scratching and screeching, knowing all the while that you do not have the means to ignore your rats like most people do. The longer you ignore these rats in your cellar – the more they multiply. Clear out your cellar and cultivate your garden, for only then is there peace for you.

How to Clear the Rats from Your Basement

The simplest way to describe a process of clearing rats from your basement is just "shoo them out." That means you just "get out" (express) every "rat" you encounter in your consciousness.

If you feel angry, don't deny it – express it. If you feel embarrassed or self-conscious, don't "play it cool." Instead, openly and publicly acknowledge your embarrassment or shyness.

There is a subtle but *very* important principle you must heed while you do this, though. You must NOT identify with any rat you are expressing. These rats are not you. They may have been living and breeding in you, but they're not you. It's like the germs of a virus that has infected your body; this virus may infect you but that doesn't make *you* the virus. You are something magnificent and beautiful that you'll discover in your basement in the absence of these rats.

If you identify with a rat – say the rat is anger – you might express some anger and at the same time think "Boy, I'm an angry person!" The moment you do that – the rat has multiplied and its offspring has been given entrance back into your basement. Always remember, you are NOT what you are expressing!

What you need to do to be fully rid of each rat is to truly forgive it. When you truly forgive something, you no longer have any attachment to where it goes from there – you have freed it from all judgment in your mind. That is what you must do as you encounter each rat – express it (bring it out into the light of full consciousness) and forgive it. And forgive yourself for judging yourself for harboring it!

Encounter Groups

Encounter groups – especially ones with skilled facilitators – are a great way to rid yourself of many rats in your basement very quickly.

An encounter group is a group of people who come together with the purpose of reaching greater honesty with each other and themselves. Organized encounter groups are often at least a few days long and involve activities designed to reveal and cast out the rats in participants' basements. As the trust level increases in the group the other people encourage you to become more genuine and in doing so you begin to relax your grip on your basement door – so the rats come pouring out. But because the group is expecting this of its members this pouring out of rats is applauded and encouraged instead of stifled the way it usually is in our everyday culture.

You will find with the caring support of an encounter group you can purge years' worth of rats in just a couple of days.

The qualities of a good encounter group are that it encourages:

+ *Honesty*

+ *Spontaneity*

+ *Trust in the process*

The Fallacy of Self-Determination

Now that you realize that you have a basement, you must also begin to notice that your basement is the foundation of your being – meaning *it* is what will determine your lot in life (pun intended).

Have you ever wondered why no matter how hard you consciously try to "change your life" there seems to be some invisible and overwhelming force inside you that pays virtually no mind to what your ego wants – it just moves you according to its whims? Well, that's your basement, your foundation, your unconscious mind and it is what directs your destiny – not your ego. Your ego, being self-deceived and lusting after control will try to make it seem like you have conscious control of your life – but you don't. That's just an illusion – an ego-centric delusion.

Your unconscious mind is vastly more powerful than your conscious mind, which is the domain of the ego (or self concept). To presume to be able to determine your ego self and have that ego self determine your destiny is a fallacy that your unconscious mind will gladly toy with.

If you want to influence your life in a positive way you must purge your unconscious mind of the rats of guilt (self hatred). Then, because your unconscious mind will be free of self-hatred it will bless you with the joyous situations of self–love.

Remember it is your vast unconscious mind that determines your fate. You must learn to love your fate as a way of learning to love your unconscious mind, which in the end is part of your true being.

Amor Fati

Nietzche writes about the love of your fate – "amor fati." It is experienced during that moment of surrender when you dislocate from the wants of your ego and actually want what your soul wants. In this instant you feel the ecstasy of stepping away from your ego and becoming wide awake.

Free Will – A Story of Recovery

"A choice made out of ignorance is not choice.
It is the most effective and subtle way
to empower one's enemies."
~ Sun Tzu, The Art of War

Will grew up in a traditional American household. His parents stayed married. They lived in the suburbs. They could afford to send him to college. He was one of the "lucky" ones to have the things he had as a child.

When Will was three years old, he fell off his tricycle. His dad was right there. His dad could have comforted him, but he didn't. He didn't know how. Instead of acknowledging Will's pain and sadness, Will's dad just wanted to fix him up. "C'mon. You're tough." he said, "Don't cry." He dusted Will off, patted him on the back and tried to teach him to be "tough" by burying his feelings.

This event was Will's first memory.

When Will needed a hug from his father, his father was uncomfortable with intimacy. When Will needed understanding from his father, his father didn't understand empathy. When Will needed his dad to be there with him in the pain and disappointment of falling off his tricycle, his dad just couldn't go there.

As Will grew up, he experienced many incidents with his dad, just like the tricycle fall. Every time the responses were the same. Will would be overwhelmed with feeling and his dad would become very uncomfortable and resort to trying to help Will stop all those "unhappy" feelings. Every time this happened, Will became more and more uncomfortable with his feelings, just like dad.

When Will was four he watched his dad give flowers to his mom when he got home from work some days. He knew how much his mom loved getting flowers from dad. He could sense the love she felt because of them.

One day Will's mom seemed particularly upset. That loving way about her just wasn't available. Will was struck with the impulse to bring her some flowers so she could feel that love again.

He ran across the yard to the neighbors' garden and saw all sorts of chrysanthemums, daffodils, and daisies. He also found tulips sprouting from the ground, all in a neat row. "Oooh, how wonderful!" he beamed to himself, "Mom is going to be so happy when I bring her all of these flowers."

Diligently and earnestly, will reached with his tender little hands and grabbed stem after stem. He had to use all his strength to detach the flowers from their roots. Eventually his arms were overflowing with his bouquet of freshly picked flowers. Will, feeling quite satisfied, ran back home to give them to his mom.

He was so excited to give all the beautiful flowers to his mom, that when he got to the door he forgot to take off his shoes. They were caked with dirt and mud from the garden. Obliviously, he ran through the house calling in his squeaky little voice, "Mommy! – … Mommy! - …"

All of the sudden he heard a scream from behind him, "William Jeffery Lawrence! What in God's name have you done?!!! You stupid little brat!" She hollered as she closed in, "Who do you think you are destroying Mrs. Smith's garden like that?! She is going to be furious! And now look what you've done to our new carpet!! You have ruined it!!! How many times have I told you to take your shoes off in the house?!!!" she screamed hysterically as she hovered over him spanking him frenziedly, "Go to your room!! And take off your shoes, damn-it!"

Will was crushed. He went up to his room and buried his face in his pillow and sobbed for over an hour.

Will had been earnestly following his impulse to offer love and joy to his mother, but the reaction he encountered was overwhelming anger and hostility. "What is happening?" his little heart silently wondered as he endured his mother's wrath. Overwhelmed with shame, Will began to hate himself for making his mom so unhappy.

As Will grew up, he experienced many incidents like this with his mom; and also with relatives and peers. Whenever he would trustingly follow an impulse to express loving he would be met with merciless shaming. It didn't take long for Will to begin to distrust those impulses to be loving towards others. It just felt safer for him to hold them inside.

By the time he was twenty, Will was no longer free. He no longer trusted his feelings or his impulses. All he could trust were the rules of conduct that had been beaten into him. He became imprisoned by the conditioning of his childhood.

Will's curriculum is not unique. Almost all of us have been through it. And almost all of us continue to suffer, to this day, because of it.

Will matured from a free feeling, impulsive child into a frozen, tough and withdrawn adult. Will's feelings were well repressed and his actions became calculated. He knew how to get the kinds of responses that he wanted and that's what he did. He got approval from people whom he wanted to please, because he did what was expected and "responsible." He got good at this game.

Now instead of love being his inspiration, just making life work his way and winning became his ambitions.

He still had memories of the effervescent sparkle of his youth, but they were well dulled. Deep down he longed for the innocent playful joy of his childhood, but he was resigned to the notion that it would be impossible to have it back, or at very least, completely irresponsible. He would never go there again.

Well into his mid-life, Will knew nothing of his soul. He cowered in fear, he robbed, he cheated and he lied his way through life – all in the name of winning. He was no criminal, because he did all of his robbing, cheating and lying legally - in the vast ethically neutral arena of business. If he committed any crimes they were spiritual crimes. Only Will never suspected that he was doing anything wrong. He saw himself as a "good person." He read self help books and meditated. He ate vegetarian food and recycled. He spent years "improving" himself. Sure it was a bit narcissistic, he would freely admit, "but it was essential to succeeding," he would argue.

Will had no real friends. He only invested his precious time and energy with people he felt he could gain from materially. Will was determined to get ahead at all costs. People lost their humanity in his mind and were seen as merely assets or liabilities. Opportunities for exercising compassion and tenderness in his dealings were eclipsed by his intense focus on doing only what was guaranteed to "work." This attitude led Will down some pretty dark passages in his middle years.

During this period of intense ambition, Will chose more and more not to trust life, including anything or anyone in it. More than that, he was slowly discovering that he could not even trust himself.

Will preferred control anyway. He didn't need trust if he could just control things – and people too for that matter. So for a period, Will chose to seek control instead of trust at every pass. He even developed a gleeful satisfaction in how easy it was for him to wrestle control away from others.

Will did win a great deal of control and he grew quite rich and powerful. His career had become his drug of choice. After all, his life was pretty sad and lonely when he wasn't playing "the big shot" in the business world. His relationships were increasingly shallow, empty and abusive.

The pain of facing the enormous lack of intimacy in his life, often led him to drink and womanize. When he felt rejected, he would go into a binge, eating everything in sight. He would tell himself that he "deserved it," because of how hard he worked, as he packed down hamburgers, pizza and ice cream. Other times, when he felt lonely he would binge on sex or fantasy; spending himself into a mild coma. His hedonistic habits started to own him, and everything he did started to have a frantic compulsive quality about it.

Will started becoming fat and old ahead of his time. Each day felt more like hell than the last. "What is happening to me?" he thought. He was so good at being "in control," but now he could hardly control himself. Every morning, after a night of binge drinking, binge eating, chain smoking, and emotionless sex, he would wake up angry with himself.

Every morning he would say "That's it, I'm going to get control of my life today." Only he would repeat the whole sad episode all over again that next night.

Something was wrong. As much as he wanted to stop his bad habits, there was some irresistible force inside him that would build and build and build until he crumbled under the pressure and went for a "fix" to escape it.

He knew this stuff was ruining his life, but there was something much stronger than him, inside him, driving him over the edge again and again and again. He couldn't seem to stop the momentum of the day no matter how hard he tried. He felt desperate.

That is, until a miracle happened. One day Will decided he was just going to be honest. He was tired of bullshitting his way through life. He was great at getting his way by pretending to be something he wasn't or pretending things were different than they really were. From then on, he was just going to be himself and tell it like it is, no matter how scary that was – no matter how risky that was to his career or his popularity or his relationships.

This took great self-forgiveness. Will used to deceive himself and others because somewhere along the way he decided the real Will was just not good enough. He had developed an artificial "Will," a persona that served as a charade that he could use to gain admiration and prestige. The trouble was that no one could ever truly love this artificial "Will" that he presented to the world, because it wasn't real – it wasn't really him. All that time that Will played this charade he gained much admiration and prestige but he never had love. Any time someone approached him with genuine love, he unconsciously deflected it on the basis that that love was intended for his persona, not him. Will didn't believe he deserved love, in fact Will hated himself.

Through the grace of self-forgiveness Will began to see the goodness and innocence in himself beyond all of his sad confusion and bad behavior. When Will finally started allowing himself to be genuine and natural he discovered a subtle and humble beauty about just being honest. And whenever one of his honest actions led him to experience "negative" responses from the world, he forgave himself for any judgments like, "I shouldn't have!" on the recognition that the real victory was his honesty.

With the release of energy from the forgiveness of each self-judgment, Will could see his genuine impulses more clearly. He didn't try to change them. He just observed what his impulses led him to. Soon, through his greater awareness of his impulses, he noticed a pattern. Whenever he had an impulse, to be more honest or trusting or loving, and he ignored it, he would soon begin to feel an irresistible compulsive need to eat, or drink, or have sex.

Will tried following his impulses instead of ignoring them. Many times following his impulses involved doing things that were way outside of Will's comfort zone. It meant letting go of control, becoming vulnerable again and trusting. His impulses led him to stretch his comfort zone over and over again, confronting his fears of intimacy, honesty, openness and spontaneity. He found himself being more transparent, more vulnerable and sharing more of himself with others. When he did, he saw how well received he was, and he would get a burst of enthusiastic energy. Will was starting to feel alive again – thanks to his relinquishment of the guilt of deception.

However, every now and then Will would allow himself to be open, honest and vulnerable and he would get shot down or shamed. At first these disappointments would upset Will, and holding the upset in, soon he would find himself in binge mode again. He didn't judge himself for binging though, he just watched himself do what he did, and he forgave it. As Will watched and observed the feelings that led to his binges more honestly, he realized that he never really let himself express his hurt, his sadness and his disappointment. So Will began to let it out. He let himself scream. He let himself cry. He let himself beat a punching bag or pillow. He let himself weep.

Will was surprised to discover that there were so many hurts he had never let himself face. Now, one by one, he was facing them and allowing himself to go through all the emotions that came with them. He created a safe environment in his home where he could trust his feelings and express them any way he needed to, without the fear of judgment or shame. For a whole year Will seemed to cry almost every day over a loss, a hurt or a slight he had not had the chance to mourn from his childhood, from his father and his mother. The memories of his youth weren't so dull anymore. He was becoming whole again.

Will also recognized that he needed to have a separation from his parents. Although he would only see them every few weeks, that became too much. He recognized that he would always feel terrible and regress to his old habits after being around them. He would often feel closed, ashamed, withdrawn, and driven to prove himself again for days after their visits or phone calls. This was getting in the way of his healing, and Will finally saw it for what it was.

So, courageously Will initiated a temporary separation from his folks. His mom took it pretty hard. She made it personal and she tried to use guilt as a ploy to manipulate him back under her influence. His dad acted like he didn't care, which only hurt Will more because all he ever wanted was to be important to his dad. But Will stood strong, and trusted the inner wisdom that told him this was the best thing for him to do.

Once he was out from under his childhood dependencies and patterns with his folks, Will blossomed. He felt stronger, more respectful and more intimate with others. He was able to see that many of his insecurities, blocks and neurosis were not his at all, they were merely relics passed down to him from his parents. Will was finally able to let a lot of that baggage go.

Eventually Will made an amazing discovery. All of that conflict inside him was beginning to dissipate. He would feel an impulse and he would trust himself to express it. He would have an emotion and he would let it out. His didn't need to stop it. He had made friends with his spontaneity and humanness. Those impulses, when fought, would build inside him until they overpowered him and compelled him to compulsive behavior and self abuse. But those impulses were actually a good thing if he just let them out and didn't try to control them. When he just let them be what they were and trusted their spontaneity, the impulses helped him express himself gently, lovingly and honestly. The impulses helped him deepen his relationships and discover his divine creativity.

All those times he had denied his impulses, they snowballed into a destructive pressure that would inevitably get the better of him. But now that he had the awareness and fortitude to trust his impulses, they began to work miracles through him.

There was new effervescence and sparkle to Will's life. His days were filled with the beautiful awareness of innocence and a lighthearted playfulness. He allowed his spontaneous impulses to lead him to do the most miraculous things.

Will had become free again.

Thanks to forgiveness.

The Need for Encounter

The neurotic DaVinci type needs to learn to use the outer world therapeutically as opposed to trying to avoid or control it.

Emotional Honesty

"God allows us to experience the low points of life in order to teach us lessons we could not learn in any other way. The way we learn those lessons is not to deny the feelings but to find the meanings underlying them."

~ Stanley Lindquist

Nowadays our culture seems to have veered towards promoting affectlessness – meaning we collectively are under group pressure to minimize our emotional response to our experiences. This is what it means to be "cool".

Maybe this is an artifact of our cultural overemphasis on appearance as opposed to content and our esteem for the appearance of neutrality. Genuine emotional neutrality is an accomplishment that is often exhibited in great leaders, but that genuine neutrality comes through intense encounter and maturation through the crucible of experience. This maturation into genuine neutrality actually exposes true will and makes it more accessible and potent.

"Wisdom is the daughter of experience."

~ Leonardo da Vinci

When we are "playing it cool" or being politically-correct we are usually artificially minimizing the possibility of being emotionally affected by our experiences, in an attempt to appear more evolved than we actually are. However, in actuality, we are distancing ourselves from the objects of our experience – the very encounter which used to excite our affection and our true will.

Judgment is dishonest.

"Nothing can be loved or hated
unless it is first known."

~ Leonardo da Vinci

Every moment in your life can become the most inexplicably powerful encounter with creation.

The things that keep you away from these powerful encounters with life are your unresolved emotional hurts. You've had formative experiences that so upset you, you shut down emotionally in that area of your awareness, because you deemed it unsafe. Now whenever you are required to participate in that area of your awareness again it evokes that trepidation and you shut down your true alpha/theta emotional centers and go into a superficial beta level simulation of what you've taught yourself is the only safe reaction to a situation like that. Notice you are now in your reactive mind, no longer able to respond openly and appropriately (with regard to your true wants) in those situations.

Basically, it is judgment that got you here. At some point you took on a judgment about something and from then on forward – until you forgive that judgment – you are forever removed from experiencing a powerful encounter with that aspect of your life.

As you grow older and you accumulate judgments about every little nuance of your existence, you become increasingly closed-off from genuine encounter experiences. You live your life more and more like a lifeless droid condemned to your past programming, condemned to never taste each moment in life freshly, but to only simulate for yourself a sense of "taste" generated purely from the memory of something similar. You are no longer in the moment, but in a fog of your own making – of your own judgments. Life grows increasingly dull and meaningless in this state and despair becomes the overwhelming feeling here.

"You do ill to praise, but worse to censure, what
you do not understand"

~ Leonardo da Vinci

The choice to judge rather than to know is the cause of the loss of peace. Judgment is the process on which illusions but not knowledge rests.

Judgment always involves rejection. It never emphasizes only the positive aspects of what is judged, whether in you or in others. What has been perceived and rejected, or judged and found wanting, remains in your unconscious mind because it has been perceived.

Judgment Halts Genuine Encounter

"Experience does not ever err; it is only your
judgment that errs in promising itself results
which are not caused by your experiments"

~ Leonardo da Vinci

One of the illusions from which we suffer is the belief that what we have judged against has no effect. This cannot be true unless you also believe that what you judged against does not exist, but we do not believe this, or we would not have judged against it in the first place.

In the end it does not matter whether your judgment is right or wrong. Either way you are placing your belief in the unreal – removing yourself from genuine encounter. This cannot be avoided in any type of judgment, because it implies the belief that experience is yours to select *from*.

You have no idea of the tremendous release and deep peace that comes from meeting yourself, situations and others totally without judgment. When you recognize what life is, you will realize that judging it in any way is without meaning. In fact, life's meaning is lost to you precisely *when you are* judging it.

"The truth of things is the chief nutriment of superior intellects."

~ Leonardo da Vinci

All uncertainty comes from the belief that you are under the coercion of judgment. You do not need judgment to organize your life – because it is your unconscious mind that dictates the course of your life anyway – and you certainly do not need judgment to organize yourself.

In the presence of true knowledge, all judgment is automatically suspended, and this is the process that enables genius to replace mediocrity.

You are very fearful of everything you have perceived but have refused to accept. These are the rats in your basement. You believe that, because you have refused to accept them, you have lost control over them. This is why you see them in nightmares, or in the pleasant disguises that seem to be your happier dreams.

Nothing that you have refused to accept can be brought into your awareness. These rats are not dangerous in themselves, but you have made them seem dangerous to you.

When you feel tired, it is because you have judged yourself as capable of being tired. When you judge people, it is because you choose to see them as unworthy. When you judge yourself you must judge others, if only because you cannot tolerate the idea of being more unworthy than they are. All this makes you feel tired because it is essentially disheartening.

You are not really capable of being tired, but you are very capable of wearying yourself. The strain of constant judgment is virtually intolerable. It is curious that an ability so debilitating would be so deeply cherished. Yet if you wish to believe you control reality – instead of just surrendering to it – you will insist on holding on to judgment. You will also regard judgment with fear, believing that it will someday be used against you. This belief can exist only to the extent that you believe in the efficacy of judgment as a weapon of defense for your own ego's authority over the unconscious mind.[18]

Non-Judgment = Encounter + Energy!

I have a two and a half year old son. He is the happiest, most exuberant, playful, energetic, enthusiastic child I have ever known. He is almost perpetually enjoying his own little party. To him every moment is an opportunity to jump, dance, sing, yell, throw, spin, smash, and live it up. He'll run over to our clothes hamper and gleefully throw the whole thing over, dumping all of the clothes onto the floor with his sing song proclamation, "I make a mess! I make a mess!" To him a mess is a good thing. It is fun and sensual and a wonderful state to lavish in. This horrifies a part of me.

I was taught messes are "bad" and "wrong" and "irresponsible" and reflect poorly on my own self worth. There is a programmed idea in my head that screams out in horror and woe at the sight of a mess. Freud says I was potty-trained too strictly. My wife agrees.

So I'll have a "hard" day of "work." You know, making "important" phone calls and handling "urgent" situations, cleaning up or avoiding "messes" of all kinds. (Everything in quotes are judgments I have chosen to place on those experiences, in case you didn't notice.) So after a "busy" and "wearing" day of judging almost every experience that comes my way; I am "fried." The reason I exercise so much judgment at work is because somewhere along the way I was taught that I am "responsible" when I exercise "good judgment" and I am "irresponsible" when I don't bother to use my "better judgment." So I've spent decades developing a set of rules for my behavior and perception, which in one way or another have been approved as "good judgment." Remembering and playing by all those rules can be exhausting over the course of a day.

So it's eight o'clock and I am feeling fried. I don't want to interact in any more situations because I am so tired of the effort it takes each time I am compelled to judge the situation and behave accordingly. So I am stuck in business-judgment mode and I just want to vegetate in front of the TV where the only judgment left to make is what to eat and what to watch, which are relatively easy "unimportant" calls.

However my son has spent the day playing. He is just enjoying the wonder of being alive. He isn't wearied by a day of judgment. He is inspired (in-spirit) by his own attitude of playfulness and peace.

So here I am turning up the volume on the TV, doing my best to ignore and block out his exuberance. I just can't take it. It hurts to perceive, because it reminds me what a hellish day of judgment I've had by contrast. And I actually chose to have that day full of my own judgments!

Judgment is wearying. Accepting someone else's judgment of who you should be or what you should do will wear you out. If you let go of judgment, you can just observe and learn. You will naturally just follow your bliss. You may take more "risks" but you'll also have much more energy to fuel your newfound brilliance.

Forgiveness is the Elixir to Judgment

*"The essence of genius is to
know what to overlook."*

~ William James

The way back from the emotionally deadened heart of judgment is through forgiveness. Forgiveness states not that you are "wrong" or "this is wrong", but acknowledges "I do not understand." When you acknowledge that you do not understand you open the way for the truth to reveal itself to you. Truth is beauty, so if you are not seeing the beauty of a person or situation, you are not seeing the truth. There must then be a judgment in your mind blocking your experience of the present truth. Discover that judgment and forgive it, and then the beauty of the moment can reveal itself to you, showing you the truth of your own beauty in return.

Patience is of great help in the process of forgiveness. For often the reason we rush to judgment is because it is intolerable to our ego's sense of security to be left in wonder. It is our ego's disdain for wonder – for having to humbly admit "I do not understand" – that compels us to rush to judgment.

*"Patience serves as a protection against wrongs as
clothes do against cold. For if you put on more
clothes as the cold increases, it will have no power
to hurt you. So in like manner you must grow in
patience when you meet with great wrongs"*

~ Leonardo da Vinci

Encounter with Death

"While I thought that I was learning how to live,
I have been learning how to die."

~ Leonardo da Vinci

Every act of creation is an encounter with the life instinct and the death instinct. When you truly create, you are releasing your life force into the object of your creation. To a DaVinci (a 'total human') who thinks in wholes, this release of life feels total, and thus is experienced as an encounter with death.

To live fully, a DaVinci must embrace his own death. He must be willing to let himself go into the abyss of the unknown and to relish every moment as his last. It is only in this fearless dance with death that the DaVinci becomes truly alive, for he has faced his fear of death and can now experience the unencumbered joy of life.

"If you don't know how to die, don't worry;
Nature will tell you what to do on the spot, fully
and adequately. She will do this job perfectly for
you; don't bother your head about it."

~ Michel de Montaigne

The same is true about life once you accept your encounters with death honestly.

Death Anxiety

"Pain and death are part of life. To reject them is
to reject life itself."

~ Havelock Ellis

Death anxiety is due to self-deception about one's own mortality. When we deny or reject the awareness of our own eventual death, we are living in a manic state that is in effect a state of running from one's own destiny. This is accompanied by massive subconscious anxiety that traps one on the delusional side of the life and death issue.

> *"In the last analysis, it is our conception of death which decides our answers to all the questions that life puts to us"*
>
> ~ Dag Hammarskjold

Anxiety is not so much the result of a fear of something as it is the result of lying to oneself about the eventuality of that something happening. For example, it was once thought that women who were rejected by their mothers had high levels of generalized anxiety. Then it was discovered that this was only the case for middle and upper-class women. Women from poor backgrounds who were rejected by their mothers didn't seem to have generalized anxiety. It was then discovered that the key difference was that girls in poverty who were rejected by their mothers were well aware of this rejection while it was happening. Their mothers made no pretences to hide this rejection of them. That's just how it was and they got on with their lives. However, in middle and upper-class families, girls who were rejected by their mothers were also lied to about it. Their mothers secretly rejected them all-the-while pretending to love them, for the sake of appearances. These women experienced massive generalized anxiety, because their conscious mind was in fear and conflict with what their unconscious mind already knew.[19]

So it is that the fear of death may be the inhibitor to the creative act, but self-deception regarding death produces a generalized death anxiety that is a perpetual inhibitor to genuine living and enjoying a creative life.

Encounters Can Help You Focus

In order to focus for an extended period on a particular task that you need motivation for, find a distracting environment that you can block out. The stimulation of your encounter with what would seem to be a lively and distracting environment might help your mind move into a greater alpha state and fuel your focus on the task that is normally too weak on stimulation to hold your focus.

Go outside into your unconscious mind and work on your thesis amongst the buzz of life being lived - the muse will find you there and whisper in your ear your lessons for the day. For it is your encounter with life in all its forms that brings shape to that deep wellspring of ideas that is your unconscious mind. Your art is the discovery of the space (gap) where you and your unconscious finally meet.

That is why the beach or a hike in the mountains often brings such unexpected inspiration. You will do your greatest thinking amidst your most powerful encounters.

True creativity is an act of joining - of reuniting - your consciousness with a small rejected element of the unconscious. In your art you are expressing the psychic release of energy by this reunion.

Creative & Sexual Encounters

Creative encounters are similar to romantic and sexual encounters. The artist encounters something that inspires a union between subject and medium – his soul shapes the medium in its image – the offspring is art. Likewise the romantic and sexual encounter inspires a union between two people – the surrendering to the shaping of another's soul.

This is why artists – DaVinci's – are so promiscuous in nature. They are filled with the irreducible need to fill that gap between subject and object – thee & thou – you and me. We want that connection – that union – that joining – and without it we feel unspeakably alone. Our loneliness envelops us and sinks us into despair.

The only time we feel truly alive and in love is when we are partaking in the act of joining or creating – when we are swept up in the joy of a sublime encounter. Everything else pales in comparison. Everything else makes us weak. For the mere thought of not joining or creating fills our hearts with the dark primordial terror of losing God.

Some DaVincis learn to fully channel their longing into platonic acts of joining or creating – they may discover intimacy with Eros in their dreams and their creations – enough to contain the DaVinci's abundant creative/sexual impetus. But alas many DaVincis find they can only be satisfied with many romantic human encounters. We have a long history of DaVincis known to be quite promiscuous, (several recent examples include John F. Kennedy, Martin Luther King, Jr. and Bill Clinton).

The Men of Greatest Achievement Have High Sex Drives

The following is an excerpt from Napoleon Hill's classic, Think & Grow Rich:

"The emotion of sex has beneath it the possibility of three constructive potentialities, they are:

1.) The perpetuation of mankind.

2.) The maintenance of health, (as a therapy, it has no equal).

3.) The transformation of mediocrity into genius through transmutation.

Sex transmutation is simple and easily explained. It means the switching of the mind from thoughts of physical expression, to thoughts of some other nature.

Sex desire is the most powerful of human desires. When driven by this desire, men develop keenness of imagination, courage, will-power, persistence, and creative ability unknown to them at other times. So strong and impelling is the desire for sexual contact that men freely run the risk of life and reputation to indulge it. When harnessed, and redirected along other lines, this motivating force maintains all of its attributes of keenness of imagination, courage, etc., which may be used as powerful creative forces in literature, art, or in any other profession or calling, including, of course, the accumulation of riches.

The transmutation of sex energy calls for the exercise of will-power, to be sure, but the reward is worth the effort. The desire for sexual expression is inborn and natural. The desire cannot, and should not be submerged or eliminated. But it should be given an outlet through forms of expression which enrich the body, mind, and spirit of man. If not given this form of outlet, through transmutation, it will seek outlets through purely physical channels.

A river may be dammed, and its water controlled for a time, but eventually, it will force an outlet. The same is true of the emotion of sex. It may be submerged and controlled for a time, but its very nature causes it to be ever seeking means of expression. If it is not transmuted into some creative effort it will find a less worthy outlet.

Fortunate, indeed, is the person who has discovered how to give sex emotion an outlet through some form of creative effort, for he has, by that discovery, lifted himself to the status of a genius."

~ Napolean Hill "Think & Grow Rich"

The Need for a Mentor

Repeated encounters with a good artistic DaVinci mentor are most helpful in helping the young or neurotic DaVinci to find his voice. The mentor stands as an example of successfully expressed will. He serves as a template for the apprentice DaVinci to discover his own inner truth and expression of the divine will.

This mentor serves as a most tangible form of encouragement that trust in one's own creative impulses (as irrational and fearfully uncontrollable as they may seem) can have powerfully positive results.

"By a happy chance, a common theme links the lives of four of the famous masters of the High Renaissance -- Leonardo, Michelangelo, Raphael and Titian. Each began his artistic career with an apprenticeship to a painter who was already of good standing, and each took the same path of first accepting, then transcending, the influence of his first master. The first of these, Leonardo da Vinci (1452-1519), was the elder of the two Florentine masters. He was taught by Andrea del Verrocchio (1435-88), an engaging painter whose great achievement was his sculpture. Verrochio also had considerable influence on the early work of Michelangelo. Verrocchio's best-known painting is the famous Baptism of Christ, famous because the youthful Leonardo is said to have painted the dreamy and romantic angel on the far left, who compares more than favorably with the stubby lack of distinction in the master's own angel immediately beside him."[20]

Ready, Fire, Aim ...

Often the most effective and expedient way to conquer a challenging task is to "just do it." Most people have learned one way or another to do a lot of thinking and planning around actions that they are about to take which are important to them.

The obvious motivation behind this "planning" is to avoid making mistakes. The trouble is that more often than not, all the planning in the world is fruitless in avoiding error, because you rarely have all the data you need. Life is so complex and unexpected that plans are easily thwarted by "the gods."

If instead of removing yourself from a scary and immediate encounter with the object of your task, you just go for it. You will experience that powerful encounter. Most likely you will live through it, and from that experience you will have gained volumes of feedback on how to do it better next time.

Richard Branson had a mantra that helped him build his multi-billion dollar Virgin Empire ...

"Oh screw it. Let's do it!"

~ Richard Branson, DaVinci & Rebel
Billionaire CEO of Virgin

Will (Love) Vs. Apathy

"I have a very strong feeling that the opposite of
love is not hate – it's apathy."
~ *Leo Buscaglia*

Apathy is a result of disengagement with your life encounters. Playing it cool, acting politically correct, suppressing emotion, denying your truest desires all result in apathy and depression.

As our culture progresses to greater levels of honesty, people who are just playing it cool are no longer interesting or desirable. It is honesty – hot, alive and filled with the fire of emotion – that is what we now crave.

For the last 30 years, "That's cool." was the mantra of the culturally progressive; but now "that's hot" seems more inline with what we truly want to experience.

Heaven & Earth – Theta & Alpha

"The knack of flying is learning how to throw
yourself at the ground …
and miss."

~ Douglas Adams

To move beyond what is proven to the more mysterious and powerful dynamics of the esoteric world, we must take on faith as our new companion. We must trust that what the poet and mystic have to say is equally important to that of the staunch "realist".

If you are an Alpha DaVinci Type, chances are you prefer the more grounded writings of "practical," "provable" science, but I encourage you to follow in the footsteps of the great scientist Leonardo da Vinci and embrace the deep inexplicable wisdom that art can convey when it is fully surrendered to.

If you are a Theta DaVinci Type chances are you resonate more with the esoteric musings of great artists and mystics, because they describe the inner stirrings that you already know.

The greatest DaVincis – including Leonardo da Vinci and Albert Einstein have expanded their minds to become both Alpha and Theta, by appreciating both science and mysticism as relevant and helpful sources of knowledge. This is the ultimate duty of the DaVinci, to connect heaven and earth.

The Miracle Impulse

Following a genuine encounter you may experience a miracle impulse. There is a power in you that can literally save the world. There is a power in you that is so vast that you are afraid to face it. The sheer magnitude of this strength is so great compared to the littleness you have identified with that you have developed maladapted defenses in the attempt to avoid your strength. The saying "He doesn't know his own strength," applies to you and you have always suspected this to be the case.

What is the Miracle Impulse?

The miracle impulse is the force deep inside of you that has the power to literally save the world. You have always known this impulse, because it never ceases, but you may have forgotten by now how to handle it.

Often this impulse is heavily repressed and distorted, because most people are far too uncomfortable releasing this kind of power from their minds. This book is a reintroduction to your inheritance as a child of God who has the God given gift to work miracles. All you need to do is learn to recognize your miracle impulse for what it is and learn to submit yourself to the Authority within you who knows how to use it well.

Somewhere along the way your mind may have been filled with ideas that inhibited your full expression. That is okay. You can always recover. When you accept ideas that limit you, they'll do just that. When you accept ideas that liberate and strengthen you, they'll do just that.

Hopefully as a child you were not shamed away from your own deepest truth. Hopefully you are still aware of a place inside of you that you find more trustworthy than anything the world can ever show you. Hopefully you are fully aware of a fountain of spontaneous wisdom that pours forth from inside of you. But, if you have lost sight of this place, it's okay. Your miracle impulse will guide you back.

If you have lost sight of the fountain of power and healing inside of you, then you may have developed some adverse coping mechanisms to stabilize yourself. Some of the things you may use to relieve the pressure of the miracle impulse are recreational sex, masturbating, sports, drinking, compulsive gambling, overeating, picking your nose, obsessive compulsive behavior, strong habits or addictions.

If you have an "addictive personality," if you are obsessive and/or compulsive, or if you are manic-depressive you are blessed. It may not seem like it right now, but you have a gift. These conditions are symptoms of a strong, minimally repressed miracle-impulse. Your only problem is in channeling the overwhelming force of your miracle-impulses. Learning to channel your miracle-impulses constructively will take work and dedication, but the rewards to you will be vast.

The Need for Limits

*"The difference between genius and stupidity is
that genius has its limits."*

~ Anonymous

Without limits there would be no need for art, and thus no need for the artist. Limits represent death – the ultimate limit of human experience. Without death there would be no anxiety to life. Without limits there would be no impetus for art. Art is first the respect of the given limits and then the creative transcending of those limits. First is the canvas, with its implicit edges, limited and ordinary. Then the great artist comes and paints the canvas to the point that the image on the canvas becomes infinite; completely transcending the edges. But it was first the artist's encounter with those edges – those limits – that evoked the limitless in him.

The mediocre artist fills a canvas with beautiful imagery. The great artist transcends his canvas and fills the world.

Transcend your canvas and fill the world!

*"There shall be wings! If the accomplishment be
not for me, 'tis for some other."*

~ Leonardo da Vinci

The conscious mind is a limited mind – in fact the conscious mind seems to be nothing more than a tiny circle drawn in the sand of an endless beach. The unconscious mind is the beach, the ocean, the planet – everything. The unconscious mind is unlimited and unencumbered. The role of the artist is to bring the freedom and limitlessness of the unconscious mind for an instant into the realm of limits, where its artifacts shine like beacons of hope – proclaiming "Even this can be overcome! There are no limits. There is no death!"

DaVincis Are Inwardly Sensitive

DaVincis have dangerously low repression levels.

Repression is an inhibiting factor in our minds, which desensitizes us and minimizes the intensity of experiences. Repression keeps the impact of pain, joy, spontaneous impulses and empathy in check. It is a way of stabilizing our perception.

When we have little repression, we are more sensitive to the winds of our psyche; we are more compelled by the urges of our bodies; we are more subject to the deep impulses within each of us to connect with each other.

We feel more pain. We feel more joy. We may cry more, but when we laugh it is *way* more genuine. We feel hurt easily and, in turn, we might overestimate how much pain others are feeling. Our sensitivity to each other is heightened and we tend to share the emotions of those around us.

Because we repress ourselves less, we are naturally more open – and more sensitive to how open others are towards us. Often this leads to feeling terribly alone. We sense the potential depth of sharing and tenderness available in our relationships, but we witness others withholding from us – and, in turn, us from them. We like being with our family and our friends, but we are frustrated by how little they offer of themselves; and we are frustrated by how little they are willing to receive of us. So we often feel alone, even when we are with our families, with groups of our friends, or with our co-workers. It's like being in a desert, knowing there must be water somewhere – there must be intimacy somewhere.

We are thirsty for those true connections with others. Our throats are parched and blistered from all the dry emotionless conversation we engaged in. Our relationships are withering before our eyes and we don't know what to do about it. Our throats constrict to the point that we can barely continue our mechanical and lifeless negotiations with our co-workers and business associates. We have reduced everyone in our lives through our endless manipulations to get to our material goals. But what good are these goals without intimacy?

Our thirst for deep and genuine relationships has gone so long unanswered that it manifests in all sorts of anxiety. Our culture tells us that this can be cured with the latest psychoactive pill, but we are all too aware that it is our hearts not our brains that are in pain. All we truly want is to have our heart's burning thirst quenched with the living water of honest soulful sharing. It is our nature to need deep trusting connections with each other; and we have denied it too long.

When our repression is lowered, we become all too aware of the aching need in ourselves for genuine intimacy. We may feel alienated and hopeless when we can't find others who will lower their repression too, so they can experience the joy of genuine sharing with us.

We can only survive so long without the experience of deep connection. When our desire to connect is denied we feel horribly empty and pretty soon we begin to panic. Because we are so intensely sensitive to separation, not being allowed to connect is like not being allowed to breathe. We are easily upset by dishonesty and superficiality in our relationships. We become fatigued by small talk and shallow conversation, because we want the real thing. We want communion!

Impulse Sensitivity

Another catch about being sensitive is that we are also more open to our impulses. When impulses come, we may not choose to follow them, but we do *feel* them – sometimes quite intensely. Our impulses can come from different aspects of our consciousness and they can lead us to do almost anything.

Growing up we usually learn not to trust our impulses. Most of us, from the time we were potty trained, or earlier, learned that in order to be a good boy or girl and thus worthy of love we must sublimate and control our impulses. In order to satisfy this perceived requirement we develop new habits to wrestle control from our spontaneous impulses, directing energy into predictable and appropriate behavior; such as learning to always wait and get to a toilet when we have the impulse to "go."

But our bodies are not the only places where our impulses can come from.

In our culture we identify pretty strongly with our bodies. We aren't usually taught to see ourselves as souls. Every behavioral modification demanded of us reinforces the message "I am just this body and I must control myself. My impulses are not to be trusted at all."

It's easy to see how our cultural environment encourages no distinction between our bodies and our souls; between physical impulses and spiritual ones. Unfortunately when we are children we unquestioningly accept and internalize the dictates of our environment. We believe the messages telling us that our impulses are wrong. So we stop trusting our impulses. Because we experience many impulses coming from the deepest part of ourselves, we stop trusting ourselves. Our soulful expression is denied and its energy is sublimated into conformist behavior. Sometimes we rebel against conformity, but even then we are merely conforming to non-conformity.

Through our vigilance against our impulses we begin to lose our natural spontaneity. Then in our longing to "act natural" we often begin fabricating complex inner schemes and habitual dances that simulate spontaneity using rapid but very carefully pre-choreographed behavior.

Alas, in the end this never satisfies us and we search for other ways to fill the void. To fill this void, we'll try almost anything.

Addiction & Compulsion

When you deny the original action that your deep impulses impel you towards, you are blocking yourself. You are denying your own soul. You are not living anymore – you are bowing to cultural rules in a sad robotic way. You have denied yourself and others the joy of *you*.

When God gives you a miracle to perform, it is usually an act of joining fearlessly with someone. You are given the direction and the energy to perform this miracle by the divine source of life. If you refuse this call, you may be able to use your ego's will to deflect from the direction your soul calls you to, but you are still stuck with all the energy that was given you to perform that miracle. You can temporarily destroy moments of grace and force them into ego-trips – that's your choice – but that divine energy cannot be destroyed. It will tear you apart inside until you release it or squelch it.

That's where compulsions are born. There are many behavioral ways to dissipate your energy. Compulsive sex, eating, drinking, drug use, gambling, work, sport, and exercise are all appropriate at times but can be easily overdone. They are often used compulsively as culturally acceptable forms of miracle impulse deflection and suppression.

Sensitivity Meets Impulse

As DaVincis our strong impulses are complicated by our great sensitivity. With far less repression than the Normal type, we are more sensitive to the impulses that are begging us to reach out and be close to others. Often these come from our souls. But we get overly concerned with how others may react to our invitation. Our attempts to follow our impulses to join are not always met kindly by our social circles and our cultural environment.

When the pain of rejection or dismissal comes on too strong, we withdraw. This withdrawal feels like hell, and it compels us to desperately seek for some alternative form of release, or comfort, or even oblivion. When we withdraw, we disconnect the intention of the impulse from the energy behind it. But the energy of the impulse lingers in our minds. This energy is intense and disorienting when we try to control it consciously. It makes us feel antsy and makes our skin crawl.

In our withdrawal we are still stuck with the energy to do what we were intended to do as someone who is engaged and participating. This energy backs up on us and makes us crazy. The energy needs to be dissipated somehow and our minds race to find an outlet different from the one for which the energy was originally intended. This sets us into a state of anxiety or panic.

Because we're too afraid to let our impulses have their way we almost suffer the resultant depression and anxiety gladly. We soon learn coping habits to sublimate and channel all of that uncomfortable impulse energy into specific compulsive activities. Whether the compulsive activity is eating, having sex, drinking or getting high; they are all attempts to conceal the real wanting from the deepest level of our being.

Your Head versus Your Heart

The deepest level of our being is our hearts and our souls. We can experience ourselves as being our social roles, or being our body, or being our personality; but our deepest being is our heart and soul. We can experience learned impulses from all of the other levels, but the only impulses that are always truly our own are the ones from our hearts and souls.

So much of our culture is wrapped up in being brainy. We like to think a lot, and we have heady thoughts. When asked where their consciousness is centered, most people in the high-tech countries will gesture to their heads. While people from places like South America will often gesture to their hearts. This is not just a cultural idea about where consciousness comes from; it is a pervasive attitude, style of thought and way of being.

When you operate from a head centered consciousness, your ability to relate empathetically with the world is greatly hindered. Your intellectual ideas and ideals rule your mind and thus your behavior. This is not natural.

You see, your ego resides in your head. Your ego is selfish and automatic. Your ego is a sophisticated arsenal of ideas and beliefs designed to further enhance and promote a selfish agenda. The ego compels you to identify with it, but it isn't really you. It's just a bunch of beliefs about who you are … and those beliefs were most likely forced into your mind by other egos.

So when you think with your head, you are operating in the realm of the ego and it is likely you will be caught up in its cold, emotionally removed attitude. This is what makes you neurotic.

One thing the ego does is try to remove any opposing points of view. So what our brainy, science driven culture has done is undermined the belief that your heart has intelligence.

We're taught that our brains do all the thinking. Since our brains are the realm of the ego, our ego wins our allegiance that way. But is it really true that our brains are the only intelligent organ of our bodies?

Surprisingly, the answer is no. (Much thanks to Rossen Townsend and Joseph Chilton Pearce for pointing this out.)

Neurocardiologists, like J. Andrew Armour, M.D., Ph.D., have found that 60 to 65% of heart cells are actually neural cells, not muscle cells as was once believed. The heart's neural cells are identical to the neural cells found in the brain. They operate through the same connecting ganglia and use the very same kinds of neurotransmitters found in the brain.

Literally your heart has thoughts! Your heart is a sensory organ and part of the emotional response system that enables you to express emotions. Half of your heart's neural cells process information from all over your body and keep your body's processes harmonized. The rest of your heart's neural cells are connected with the emotional centers of your brain. There is a constant dialogue between your heart and your brain that your ego is not even aware of.

The responses that your heart makes affect your entire system.

Your emotions are intimately tied to your heart's electromagnetic spectrum. Biophysicists now say that your heart creates a powerful electromagnetic field. This electromagnetic field encompasses your body and extends eight to twelve feet from your heart. This electromagnetic field affects your brain by immersing it in whatever electromagnetic radio wave spectrum your heart is radiating. So your heart is literally creating the environment in which your brain thinks. These different electromagnetic wavelength environments are presumably what entrain your brain into different brainwave states and affect your thought processes dramatically.

"Groundbreaking research in the field of neurocardiology has established that the heart is a sensory organ and a sophisticated information encoding and processing center, with an extensive intrinsic nervous system sufficiently sophisticated to qualify as a 'heart brain.'"

~ J. Andrew Armour, M.D., Ph.D

But, what happens when you think with your heart?

Your Heart Knows Truth

Your heart is like a tuning fork. It resonates with truth. When your heart encounters truth it is energized and supplies greater strength to your whole being. Your heart resonates with the ring of truth. So whenever you are truthful you are strengthened by your heart.

Whenever you are being deceptive or being deceived, your heart will be out of phase (or out of tune) with that deception. Your heart only resonates with truth and thus only amplifies your actions and thoughts when they are in alignment with truth. Lies, falsehoods, or deceptions will put your thoughts in dissonance with your heart and will cause you to become weak while you hold on to that deception.

Our egos are designed to deceive. Egos are belief systems based on an idea that evolved in humans so that one human could more effectively control and deceive other humans and creatures. The idea that makes this possible is the idea of being a separate self. If you don't believe that you are a separate self with separate interests from other people and creatures, you will have no motivation to lie, deceive and control others. But at some point, humanity developed the capacity to think selfishly, and holding belief in the idea of being a separate self with separate and conflicting interests is the core of selfish thinking. Selfish thinking is what prompts one group of people to want to violently conquer and control another group of people. This behavior obviously has a massive impact on natural selection. Selfish cultures will likely conquer and destroy unselfish cultures, and thus it is the selfish egotistical cultures that spread the most aggressively.

Egos also only exist in our brains. Our hearts don't have egos. Egos have always been threatened by the truth and love that hearts promote, because truth and love are antithetical to selfishness and the idea of self is the cornerstone of the ego.

Egos used to just battle it out with the heart. Sometimes they won, sometimes they lost. More recently egos have become more sophisticated in their selfish tactics. By convincing science that only the brain can think, egos developed a culture that discredits the heart as a source of thought. Now, for the last couple hundred years only the brain – the domain of the ego – has been given any acknowledgement as a source of thought. This effectively removed the heart from the discourse of science.

This is basically what hostile government does when it wants total control of the minds of its populace. It shuts down the voice of dissention. This is usually done by eliminating free press. That's why free press is so important in order to maintain honest leadership.

Think of your heart as the free press. If you allow your free press to be ignored, you will likely run into a great deal of self-deception.

Trust Your Heart

If your heart resonates with truth, then your heart is your most honest and trustworthy source of wisdom.

Our hearts will often tell us not to be selfish and to join with others, whatever form that takes in each moment. Our heart's will is often to join in perfect communion. This perfect communion requires deep trust. The impulses coming from our heart are always asking us to join with and trust other hearts in one way or another. This makes us very uncomfortable.

Instead of just surrendering to our heart's will, we try to change it. We have been taught to be afraid of doing anything that is not "socially acceptable" or "polite" or "cool." Often trusting a heartfelt impulse to truly be open and reach out to another requires doing something ruthlessly honest and un-cool.

Following your heart's impulses is a habit. Almost all two-year-olds have this habit. That's why they can be so spontaneously adorable. That's also what provokes them to do the unexpected and "unacceptable" things. They are following the direction of their heart and their body. They are relatively untarnished by the directives of cultural and social norms, so spontaneous expression of their impulses is their sole habit.

Although diverting our heart's impulses into more acceptable, less obtrusive expressions may seem more convenient to us, it is dangerous and sad, because the expression of your heart's impulses is meant to be habitual. If you are not in the habit of spontaneity, then you are most likely reinforcing a distorted habit of expressing your heart's impulse energy in a contrived way.

We *have* to do something with the impulse energy or it will knock us over. So in order to fit in with our families and friends, we learn to adapt new channels for directing the force of our heart's impulses into more widely accepted behavior.

Often people aren't comfortable with you exuberantly running up to them and with unabashed honesty expressing whatever your heart's desire is. If, instead, you take your heart's impulse, to be loud and playful with someone, and divert it into stuffing your face with a whole pepperoni pizza, well that's perfectly fine with them. No one will say a word.

Once you have corrupted your impulses, you can be carried away by the relentless impetus left in their wake. Your heart's desires were what were intended to direct your impulse energy, but now all that energy is diverted into whichever controlled and compulsive behavior you have forced your impulse energy into. Maybe you overeat all the time, maybe you can't stop wanting sex, maybe you are an alcoholic or a drug addict, maybe gambling has clung to you. Whatever it is your compulsive habit may be, it is merely a relic of your true inspiration.

All the energy that drives you to indulge these habits was originally intended to propel you through the expression of your heart's desires. Unfortunately, your pure, spontaneous, impulsive nature may easily be corrupted into a sad fixated compulsive disease.

Beware of What the World Taught You

"By the time we have reached our thirties, forties, fifties -- what the world calls maturity -- we have established a set of rules and guidelines based on our past experiences, that we hope will guide us in reacting to the world and relating to other people. We always fall back on these. Many of them would be agreed with by most people in the world; and because most people would agree with them, we think that validates them. We don't recognize, however, that everyone in this world is insane. So you should never take what the world says as a guideline for what you should do."

~ Kenny Wapnick Ph. D

Joseph Campbell told us how the mythic adventure is a slaying of a dragon where each scale is a limit that we have accepted growing up. When we are young we are like a camel loaded down with learned limitations. Then when we become a hero our job is to slay each limitation – by transcending it – while still remaining aware of the principle that limitation was intended to reflect.

Your job as an awakening DaVinci is to shed every remnant of culturalization from your attitude and belief system. You have accepted many beliefs that are not your own and are not helping you. Start questioning everything you believe. Ask yourself with every action "Is this really me? Do I really mean this?"

As you progress in finding your true self, you will experience "callings" to pursue certain endeavors. Maybe it's a new career or new hobby, a new cause or a new family. Whatever that calling is, it will haunt you until you answer the call.

When you answer the call, your life will shift dramatically. It will be as if invisible hands are helping you lay the foundation for your new adventure. You may feel swept away into an entirely new existence. And you may feel a bit scared as everything you have learned up till now, no longer seems to serve you. Different rules apply on this journey. There seem to be different laws of time and space.

Your spontaneous impulses will often fly in the face of all the "rules and guidelines" the world agrees on. Your spontaneous impulses will liberate you to another plane of power and freedom.

One of the difficulties with being an irrepressible DaVinci is that the Normal type will subconsciously envy your freedom and the power behind your spontaneous impulses. Normal types and even neurotic DaVinci types will try to shame you for being too free. They may also be very condemning of any evidence of wounds or guilt being expressed by you.

Most people do not behave in accordance with the inner wellspring of their being – their heart and soul. Most people put on a "happy face," speak politically correctly in relation to whatever social norms there are; and behave according to a strict set of cultural rules. They do this with such vigilance that soon there is very little evidence of the living heart and soul inside that person, because their being has been overlaid with so many layers of learned behaviors, beliefs and attitudes that there is not room for any spontaneous impulses to come through. This is not living, this is hiding.

To an awakened DaVinci these people feel like robots and it is clear there is a light missing from around the tops of their heads. It is very difficult for a DaVinci to relate with these people as deeply as one would like, because they simply have closed off access to that part of themselves. They run on their social/cultural programming with such conviction that there is very little opportunity to truly affect them in any authentic way.

My recommendation is that the DaVinci avoid becoming too open and vulnerable in the presence of these hardened types, for they will subconsciously work diligently to convert you to their beliefs and shut you down too so that you will be less threatening to them. When you allow yourself to be too open and vulnerable you can unknowingly be subtly shamed into adopting their way.

The truth is, you probably already have to some degree. That's okay. That's just the condition of our present culture and The DaVinci Method will help you reverse that.

Be the Creative Type

Moving from being a neurotic DaVinci to being the artistic DaVinci, involves clearly and cleanly following your heart's impulses and doing what is the highest good in each moment through a deep trust of your being.

Trusting that deep inner wisdom, that creator inside you that knows the most artful, most perfect, most sublime action at any given moment, often involves confronting your fears of risk. Releasing your true self, allowing it to express through unabated, means allowing everything you have hid about yourself up until now to be potentially exposed in one momentary spontaneous expression.

Being willing to share that sometimes scary real you with others often involves surrendering your pride and forgiving all those judgments you hold against yourself. That means allowing your true being to be exposed. That means developing an attitude of non-defensiveness and non-duplicity.

This non-defensiveness and non-duplicity requires the kind of honesty we had when we were simple and straightforward … when we were children.

Why are children so much more honest than adults? What happens over the course of growing up is that we are indoctrinated with cultural norms, cultural rules and we're taught that our honesty is less important than fitting in with these cultural norms. And so we learn appropriate behavior as opposed to authentic behavior. You're going to be miserable if you stay in that state.

What this part of the DaVinci Method is designed to do, is help move that from appropriate, stale, compulsive behavior, (which is completely neurotic), to being authentic, gentle with yourself, natural, spontaneous, and free.

Authentic, honest, open, free and spontaneous behavior is based on a trust of your deep inner wisdom. This deep inner wisdom is beyond what you are conscious of. This means you are going to learn to follow 'crazy' impulses that lead you to do things that are often funny and obviously harmless, but well beyond your conscious ability to see the full beauty of.

You will start to do things in such a spontaneous way that you will just have to trust whatever you are doing is for the highest good, because you are honestly surrendering to the goodness of God. So a big part of getting to that point is learning to be relentlessly honest – otherwise you can be self-deceived about your motives and the genuineness of your actions.

At first, you may find that when you have just shed your first superficial level of dishonesty and started being honest, it's painful. The reason it's painful is because, all of the sudden, instead of getting the approval or positive feedback – that you are accustomed to getting by doing socially acceptable or socially appropriate, compulsive behaviors – you will be behaving in a less socially acceptable way. Instead of being subtle, manipulative, and duplicitous, you will be fearless and direct.

Now, you might find that you get a lot of really positive feedback, the likes of which you may have never had. Some people will be quite grateful for your honesty, but they may not tell you this until literally years later.

Meanwhile, you are probably also going to ruffle some feathers. You may experience, all over again, the same kind of shaming that you endured as a child. The kind of shaming that made you stop being honest and start being neurotic in the first place.

Shamers are the self appointed guardians of the status quo. People who are shamers use shame to put down people who operate outside of their subjective rulebook. They will say things to you subtlety – or not so subtlety – that will attempt to put you in your place, attempt to make you feel shame for your honest behavior or for being who you really are. The truth is, shamers are threatened by your greatness.

During this process you will probably encounter a good number of shamers. What you need to do to protect your process, of becoming more honest and free, is to recognize when someone is trying to shame you and respond accordingly. Realize that shaming is the most pathetic thing one human being can do to another. Shaming is saying you are worthless, because it is calling you on something you say or do and saying you do not deserve to be that free – you are worth less.

When someone tries to shame you, that doesn't mean you have to be shamed. If you can realize that their shaming attempt is about their own low self-esteem and their jealousy of your apparent freedom, you can stay calm in the presence of their shaming attempt and put it back in their laps. If you're feeling particularly attacked in the situation, just call it like you see it. You can say to the person who's shaming you something to the effect of "Are you trying to shame me?" or "Why are you trying to shame me?"

Shaming, because it is such a pathetic thing to do, is usually done covertly, so just calling the pathetic action out into the open with a direct statement or question will usually put an end to it immediately. Saying something open and direct will move the game above the table where it will dissolve – like the vampire that it is – in the light of day.

Just by being honest enough to bring that action into the open, what you are doing is you are eliminating the subversive sneak attack. You bring it out into the open and say this is not going to be unnoticed. It's being noticed what you're doing here and often that will be plenty.

Meanwhile, it's part of your work because your job is to be direct and honest. So if you're feeling someone shaming you, by all means say it honestly.

When you are going through this healing process of becoming ruthlessly and relentlessly honest, eventually you will reach a point where your honesty runs so deep that expressing your spontaneous impulses becomes natural for you again. What you'll find is that your life has been filled with grace.

When you are living a life of honesty, grace is given to you. You are allowing divine inspiration to live through you and the only way you can achieve that level of being is to become so honest and so clear that as your heart prompts you, you have the honesty and the courage to express the miracles of love that you are now sensitive to the calling for.

Recognize that by doing this, it's not just a service to you; it's a service to everyone who you relate to because everyone benefits from your honesty. Everyone benefits from your authenticity because when you are being authentic, you're not being manipulative.

A big problem with our culture – the way it's set up – is we are taught from a young age how to manipulate our behaviors and other people's behaviors through socially acceptable dances. These dances hide the true malevolence of deception under the guise of social niceties.

When you do something that's "nice for someone" it's manipulative if it isn't a genuine selfless expression of your desire to be helpful. Often being nice is an underhanded way of manipulating people into liking you. That's no genuine devotion and it does neither you nor the receiver any actual good.

When you follow your heart and follow the truest impulses of your soul – when you have a spark of compassion for someone and you follow that compassion – in that one moment you are being completely loving and grace befalls you. Those moments aren't manipulative because you're not doing it for an outcome, you're not doing it because that's what you were trained to do to be polite, you're doing it because that's what's right in the moment – and great beauty comes from those genuine acts of kindness and courage.

A large part of The DaVinci Method is learning to become relentlessly honest with yourself and with others. This takes much practice because, practically speaking, all of the sudden becoming relentlessly honest – after decades of building your life around subtle deceptions – can get you in a lot of hot water. All I can say with regard to this dilemma is that, no matter how much short term trouble you might get in, you only have so many years on this planet. So don't waste too much time getting out of the habits of the dishonest neurotic DaVinci type and into the habits of the honest productive DaVinci type (the Artist).

Also it's important to realize that 99% of your deceptions are self-deceptions. You don't even really know the truth. So simply falling into the charade of being relentlessly honest, but only superficially can have all kinds of negative affects.

You can only imagine what would happen if you just said whatever was on your mind to anyone and everyone and started behaving without any real boundaries, tact or discipline. That's not what we're talking about. That doesn't work usually.

What you need to learn through this honesty work is to be not only literally honest with your words, but more importantly to be emotionally honest. It's not just about being intellectually honest, or being transparent, it's about being great and greatness requires great emotional honesty.

To say, "I think you're fat," or "I think you're ugly," or "I don't like you" or "I think you're hot" all can have negative effects. If you say any of these without sufficient emotional maturity and honesty, you are probably shooting yourself in the foot. That's because all of those things are just surface level. They are very superficial levels of honesty.

There's deeper honesty that you need to get to and that deeper honesty involves your feelings. How do you feel about yourself right now? Are you feeling guilty about yourself? Are you loving yourself? How are you feeling about other people? Do you feel genuine devotion and gratitude for those people? Or do you feel like they have something you want that you are trying to manipulate for and get?

Those deeper emotional awarenesses discovered through honesty are the ones that you need to become in touch with and be able to express authentically because if you just want something from someone, sometimes the best thing to do in that situation for yourself is to be honest about it. By being honest about it with a sense of humor, you'll get to experience the effects of that, and you'll get to grow from it.

But if you hide your agenda, if you conceal an intention and try to run a charade being kind to someone, because deep down inside you want their approval or their attention or something that they have, if you're not honest with yourself about these things then you are being self-deceived and you're stunting your growth as an artist, as a true creator. Self deception stunts your ability to become a great DaVinci.

To be a great DaVinci you must be relentless in your honesty, pure in your action, full of integrity throughout your entire being, in everything from what you feel and what you say to what you do.

All of it will be in alignment when you reach 100% honesty. Once you're in 100% alignment, you will know because you'll have incredible power, because you're not holding back. You're not trying to deceive anyone, not even yourself.

The Self-Deception Gene

"The greatest deception men suffer
is from their own opinions."

~ Leonardo da Vinci

According to Robert Trivers, an acclaimed evolutionary biologist, there are two levels of deception that have been evolved in us. One is just surface deception, the ability to tell a lie or to do something to intentionally deceive someone else. This level of deception we are all pretty aware of.

As humanity evolved, people became better and better at sensing when someone was trying to deceive them. They would subconsciously notice the liar's eyes darting, their pulse quicken, their breathing become more rapid, or any myriad of nervous ticks that accompany the act of deception. Eventually the classic approach to lying wasn't convincing enough.

What's astounding is Robert Trivers' conviction that then there was an evolutionary advantage to becoming self-deceptive in order to lie more convincingly. (Trivers has a book coming out in late 2005 that goes into great detail about this.)

Think about it. If you want to deceive others most convincingly, the best way to do it is to believe what you are trying to convince them of yourself. So if you want to convince others of a lie that will ensure your survival, the best way to do it is to get yourself to believe the lie.

Suddenly, those who are sensitive to the evidence of someone lying can't detect that you're lying because *you* don't even know that you're lying. You believe your own self-benefiting lies.

Any lie detector test or anyone who's just aware of the subtle body language that goes along with lying would be able to pick up on it and would thus either consciously or subconsciously distrust you. However, when you believe the lie yourself, then you don't have the quickening pulse, the darting eyes, the nervous ticks and twitches, the vocal intonations and mannerisms of someone who's trying to deceive.

Now how do you convince yourself of your own lie?

The trick is to have a very powerful imagination. If a human being could develop an imagination that was so visceral, so life-like, that when they imagined a situation, they literally experienced themselves as being there, then they could concoct all kinds of fantasies that served their selfish purposes. Then they could convincingly describe their imagined experience as if it really happened.

This, unfortunately, is the ability of DaVincis.

DaVincis & Eidetic Imagery

DaVincis may all be what psychologists call *eidetic imagers.* (Eidetic is pronounced "eye-DETT-ick.") This means that you have the capacity to imagine and visualize imagery that is bright, clear, full-color, multi-dimensional and immersive.

Normal types do not do this. When they imagine something it is usually colorless and two-dimensional.

Eidetic visualization is similar to having a photographic memory and it requires high levels of Theta functioning. DaVinci types who tend to have more Theta will probably have an easier time generating eidetic images in their minds. This ability to harness eidetic imagery presents a huge double edged sword for DaVincis.

So let's tackle the downside first. Eidetic imagery can be used by your imagination to mock-up incredibly immersive scenarios. In these scenarios you can experience what that scenario would be like and even convince yourself that this eidetic experience you're having is real. You can literally manufacture your own life experiences this way. It's fantasy on steroids.

The trouble is that you can use eidetic imagery to so distort the truth in your own mind that you start believing your own fantasy. Then you can start selling this self-deception like it's the truth. Others will believe it, because there's no evidence in your delivery that you're lying – that's because you now believe your own lies.

This is a very powerful dark-magic that has been used to deceive many people.

Adolph Hitler is an infamous example of how one could use his own powers of eidetic imagery to convince an entire nation of his own self-deceptions.

Jacques Lusseyran was a blind spy for the French resistance during Adolph Hitler's reign. He was a great spy, despite his blindness, because he always knew when he was being lied to. He could hear whether someone was telling the truth or lying by the subtle difference it would make in the intonation of their voice. This is obviously a great asset for a spy to have.

Jacques Lusseyran tells the story of how horrified he was when he first heard Adolph Hitler giving a speech on the radio. He knew then that this man had a terrifying power because of the things Hitler could say, without any evidence in the intonation of his voice that he was lying.

(You can read more about Jacques Lusseyran in his beautiful spiritual autobiography **And There Was Light**.)

The issue with self-deception is that it's completely destructive to both yourself and to others. It's an abomination of the truth. You lose track of what's true and false and you don't even know anymore when you're lying. You become increasingly sociopathic when you allow your own fantasies with eidetic imagery to cloud your perception of truth. You get so removed from what's true and good in yourself that you can become completely lost.

What The DaVinci Method is designed to do is help you discover these self-deceptions in yourself and root them out. Although there may be certain political, business and negotiating advantages to being a good liar, the skill comes with its share of negative baggage. The baggage that we are concerned about in The DaVinci Method is neuroticism which is based on self deception. Essentially a neurotic DaVinci is a self-deceived DaVinci. A neurotic DaVinci has lost track of his own genuine identity and is living out a lie.

The key to your true brilliance is honesty.

> *"First and last,*
> *what is demanded of genius is love of truth."*

~ Johann Wolfgang von Goethe

Leonardo da Vinci, like Sigmund Freud and many other greats accomplished their greatness through their deep honesty. Many of Freud's and da Vinci's works are uncomfortably honest for many people to take – such as Freud's descriptions of the dark wishes of the ego, the death wish and the oedipal wish or da Vinci's courageous and scary willingness to dissect and draw the inner workings of the human body.

Courage is a precursor to great honesty and both of these geniuses had the courage to discover things the rest of humanity had proven too timid to unearth.

> *"Beyond a doubt truth bears the same relation to*
> *falsehood as light to darkness."*

~ Leonardo da Vinci

Your Subconscious Gatekeeper

Our sense system is literally bombarded with terabytes of information every moment. It would be completely overwhelming to be aware of every little nuance – every scrap of sensory information at any given moment.

> *"Our brains process **400 Billion** bits of*
> *information every second, but we are generally*
> *only aware of 2,000 of those bits."*

~ Film: "What the Bleep do we know?"

Our minds have developed ways of handling all that information. The subconscious mind filters this data and only keeps in conscious awareness the data that appears to be most self-serving.

The unconscious mind then serves as the repository of all the information that has been rejected by consciousness.

The subconscious mind then is like a gatekeeper for your consciousness. It only allows your conscious mind to sense what you have already told it is helpful for you to be aware of.

Here's a true story about how powerful your subconscious mind really is in making sure you only sense what you expect to sense.

When Columbus landed in the Caribbean, the natives literally could not see his ships. These natives' subconscious minds had no reference point for any boat as huge as Columbus's clipper ships. So when they looked towards these ships, their subconscious minds would censor out this incomprehensible information. Thus their subconscious preconceptions of what was possible would not allow them to see the ships.[21]

Then the shaman of the tribe (the DaVinci) noticed ripples out in the ocean but couldn't see what was causing them. His well honed intuition kept telling him to pay attention to that. For days and days, this shaman followed his intuition and focused on the potential origin of these ripples. Finally the shaman was able to use his eidetic imagination to mock-up something close enough to what a clipper ship looked like for his subconscious to grab hold of it. Then it let the image of the real clipper ships break into his awareness. He was finally able to see the clipper ships!

Once he saw the ships the shaman could help others see them too, by guiding their perception. This required the trust and credibility that he already had with his people.

Subconscious Programming

You can program your subconscious mind with eidetic imagery, because your subconscious mind does not know the difference between experiences you mock-up with your imagination and experiences you really have. Both experiences look equally real to your subconscious mind.

Scientists have done experiments where they put eidetic subjects into a PET scan and have them look at an object or image. They look at the areas of the brain that light up and are activated by the sight of that image. They then take the image away and ask the subjects to close their eyes and imagine that image. When the subjects do this – simply imagining the image lights up and activates the same regions of their brains again.

So every time you imagine something eidetically, your subconscious responds as if it were really happening. This is how you can work yourself up emotionally – which is a subconscious activity – just by what you think about. It is also why you have to be careful about what you make your subconscious mind believe reality is.

If you program your subconscious mind with too much fantasy, you may find that your physical and emotional reactions to things become wildly ineffective. This is a primary difficulty for neurotic Theta DaVinci types, because they tend to use fantasy to escape their fears, instead of facing them.

Getting Good Feedback past Your Subconscious

One of the most important things you need in order to get good at achieving a specific goal is timely and accurate feedback. This feedback lets you know how your thoughts and actions are helping or hindering your accomplishment of that goal.

Good feedback is readily available in most situations. However, when you are neurotic, your subconscious mind filters all the feedback you get through the lens of any self-deceived fantasies you have programmed it with. Not even honest, helpful and appropriate feedback can help you, because the feedback you're getting is being distorted through the lens of your self-deceptive stories.

Remember, all the feedback you get is filtered by the gate-keepers of your deluded subconscious, (which has been programmed by whatever eidetic imagery you've been mocking-up in your mind).

If you've allowed yourself to indulge in self-deceptive fantasies, then after a while, only feedback that reinforces your delusions is even allowed into your conscious awareness. These self reinforcing lies make you less and less effective and less aware of what would really work for you in your situation. These fantasies can become so confusing that you even forget what it is you really want in life.

You could live out your entire life chasing after something that you don't really want; all because at some point you started mocking-up fantasies that so confused you that they made you want other things.

Imagine this: You really want something so you try to go after it honestly and that doesn't work. So then you try lying to get it and that still doesn't work, because your lie isn't convincing – everybody knows you're just trying to get the thing you want. Finally, you decide to mock-up in your mind an image of your being the kind of person who would want something other than you really do so you can get closer to what you really want undetected. You immerse yourself in this fantasy of wanting that something else until you actually think you want that.

Now you have entered a world of self-deception where you actually start to believe that you are someone other than who you really are. People treat you differently now and maybe you actually get closer to that thing you originally wanted. But you no longer remember you want that now.

As soon as you enact this kind of self-deception, you quickly lose awareness of what you really want. You start hopelessly chasing goals that will never fulfill you.

Some popular substitute goals are status, money, power, a house in a particular location, a nice kind of car, a nice kind of job, a nice kind of romantic partner, etc.

You can make up all these stories about what you want and think that's going to do it for you. You can make yourself believe, "I'm going to be happy when I finally have that." But when you are self-deceived all your substitute wants are merely defenses against the fear of never getting what you really want.

Maybe all you really want is to be loved. Maybe all you really want is to feel cherished. Maybe what you really want is to feel free. But those real wants are buried under a pile of what we'll call pseudo-wants. Those pseudo-wants are often chosen because being seen as wanting those things seems to get you closer to what you really want.

Let's say all I really want is to feel valuable. I look around me and I see that people who are rich and famous get treated like they are more valuable than others. So you create a pseudo-want – you figure then, "I want to be rich and famous." And as you start pursuing that you realize that it's not easy to get rich and famous by just going directly after that. So you develop another pseudo-want that you believe will help you get rich and famous. You decide, "I want to be a rock star." And then you start pursuing that and you realize you need to have another want to get you there, so you decide, "I want to be a great guitar player." So you start really practicing the guitar, but soon you realize that – for the most part – great guitar players are "a dime a dozen." There are a million great guitar players out there and only a few of them ever get rich and famous. Now you've spent so much time trying to get rich and famous that you forgot to be valuable. And all you really wanted in the first place was to feel valuable.

Do you see how adopting the self-deception of pseudo-wants can distract you from having what you really want?

You will never feel truly fulfilled until you get really honest about what it is you really want. It's usually something pretty simple. When you get clear about that, you'll find that making good choices in your life becomes pretty simple too.

You can still have goals for material things but they won't matter so much and when they don't matter so much you can be much more strategic and patient about the way you go after them. You'll be much more effective and you'll also be able to see the important things you were afraid of looking at before.

Here's an exercise to help you on your way:

This exercise is best done out-loud and preferably with a partner who you feel safe being very open with.

1) Pick something you want.

2) Say "I want _____."(whatever it is)

3) Then say "I want _____, because it will make me feel _____."

4) Then say, "What I really want is ___."

5) Take whatever you ended with wanting in step 4 and repeat step 1 using it. Keep repeating this cycle until you discover what you really, really, really want.

Don't Make Goals Too Important

When you are blindly pursuing a goal; when you have made it the most important thing in the world to you, you are likely to have a lot of fear wrapped up in not getting it. If you have a lot of fear wrapped up in not achieving a particular goal, it's going to be very difficult for you to look at anything that's telling you that you're not achieving that goal.

Any negative feedback you get about achieving a goal that you've made too important becomes threatening to you. Your subconscious emotional self may even try to block this feedback. There's a big problem with that.

If that goal becomes so important that any time you get negative feedback or feedback that tells you that you're off course, you are likely to go into denial. Denial seems a lot easier than facing the scary realization that you are not reaching your goal the way you've been going about it.

What you'll be tempted to do is keep going into denial about all the feedback that's letting you know that you're off course. When someone surrounds themselves with "yes men" that's where they are coming from.

In that denial, you are actually making it less likely that you will accomplish the very thing that you have made so important.

"The first and most important thing is to determine and accept the worst thing that can possibly happen. It's important to do this, because once you accept the worst thing that can happen, you can then stop worrying about it happening."

~ Bob Parsons, CEO of GoDaddy.com

So the way to accomplish something is to make it not fearfully important. You let yourself care, but not that much.

You care enough to look at the situation honestly and to do what it takes to get to where you want to go; but you don't care so much that you are motivated to go into denial and lie to yourself because you've become so afraid of failing.

Negative feedback can be very scary, especially if you've got the attainment that of goal wrapped up with your identity and self-worth. It's possible to wrap the accomplishment of something so closely to your identity that the possibility of not accomplishing it threatens your identity. When something threatens your identity, this threat can be felt as severely as if the threat were on your very life. When something gets to be that important you need to let go; because anything that threatens the idea of accomplishing that goal will feel like a threat to your own existence, and you will not be making clear decisions that way. This is particularly true for DaVinci types because you tend to make things "all or nothing" and you have a very powerful imagination that can run away with you.

Remember you tend to think in wholes, so what would 100% total failure on your 100% most important goal fee like? Death. Death is the archetype of 100% failure.

You don't operate at 30 percent like 9 out of 10 people do, you operate at 0-10% when you're bored or resting or you operate at 100% when you are really going after something. So when you start experiencing failure on something you're giving 100% effort to, it can feel like death, because to fail when you give 100% can subconsciously be seen as 100% failure.

Here's a possible reason that this evolved. If you are out hunting and you are failing at hunting that could literally mean death for you and your family. So the failure to reach a goal like spearing a caribou might feel like death if you're not achieving it. You might feel like you're dying and that might motivate you to keep going after that caribou – no matter what. Also when you are pushed to your max and you're cold and starving and tired, you probably can't handle any more in terms of negative feedback, so that's a helpful time for it to be blocked out.

Hopefully your regular life experience is not that precarious and that intense. However, when you consider making that "critical" sales presentation or when you think about approaching that "all important" potential soul-mate that you've got the crush on, that can feel like life and death to you because you have wrapped up so much of your identity in the outcome of that experience.

The problem with this overly serious mind-set is that you're stopping yourself from learning and growing, because you've made it too important and too scary to gather good feedback from the experience. If you can relax and have fun with these encounters in your life you'll find yourself being more open and more honest; and you'll find everything flows more easily and naturally.

There's always going to be another sales presentation opportunity, there's always going to be another chance to encounter your potential soul-mate, but if you don't start taking things less seriously and let yourself be open to feedback (no matter how humbling), you won't be able to grow and improve as easily.

When you're open to feedback and willing to learn, the next time you can do a lot better. Often the very first step in learning to accomplish a difficult goal is learning how far away you are from that goal.

Don't take your self too seriously

"A man is least himself when he speaks as himself.
Give him a mask and he will speak the truth."

~ Oscar Wilde

One way to make rapid improvements towards your goals is to stop taking your self seriously. (Yes, I'm saying your self, not yourself on purpose, because we are talking about just your ego here, not your whole being. We are just talking about the part of you that identifies with your name and your address and your career, etc.)

When you don't take your self seriously, even your most critical goals are taken less seriously too. Everything you perceive – except when you are enlightened – is perceived in relation to your self. So by taking your self less seriously, everything in your life becomes less serious, much more enjoyable and *easier*.

Your self is the identity you, your parents and your community helped shape in you from birth. This identity is not really *you*. This identity, this self, is just a random assortment of beliefs about yourself and the world that, for the most part, are untrue.

Nobody can really tell you the Truth – capital T. That kind of Truth is beyond words. So everything you've been taught – everything that has been used to program your brain into seeing yourself and your world the way you see it, is a lie. It can't be the Truth, because the Truth is beyond teaching, beyond any set of beliefs that can be taught.

Even so, aren't your beliefs a decent approximation of the truth? Or aren't your beliefs at least mostly true? Don't they at least help a bit?

Well, only if you don't take them too seriously. You could think, "I know what's happening here." Now, that thought can serve you, but only if you don't take it seriously, because if you take any thought too seriously, that's how you lock that thought in your consciousness and eliminate the opportunity for you to discover something truer. That's why people take their selves seriously ... it's a way of locking their self identity in their minds against all the feedback coming in that says "your self concept is out of whack."

If you were to use the thought, "I know what's happening here," without taking it too seriously it might help you have some playful confidence. However, if you do take it seriously, that's when you become arrogant, you miss the opportunities to learn, because you are so focused on defending your self perception of "knowing what's happening."

The same is true about your own self concept. Don't take your ideas about who you are too seriously, because they are likely to be quite flawed. You might think you know who or what you are, but all that is based on a belief in a self concept started at birth and reinforced with *very little input from you* for the first seven to twelve years of your life. Don't believe it's true!

Don't take that self that you think you are seriously. Look in the mirror and realize "That is not me – it is merely a reflection of who I think I am filtered through all of my preconceptions of how I think I look."

When you stop taking your self seriously, you open the opportunity for you to do anything – because now no spontaneous impulse will threaten your self-concept. A self-concept, not taken seriously, has very little control over your actions, because you no longer worry about violating it. You no longer worry about violating it, because it's not you anymore – it's just an idea – an idea about who you are that was given to you by your parents and your culture.

You Were Born Spontaneous and Free

You weren't born all pent-up in your self-concept and programmed to be normal and fit-in. You were born to be spontaneous and free. And you should stay that way. This is where your beauty is.

Over time you may have developed memories – mental images – that kept you "in line." These mental images are a collection of eidetic memories of all the times you behaved honestly and spontaneously and were in some way shamed or punished for that choice.

Eventually, if you develop enough negative mental imagery it will serve as an overwhelming case against your choosing to be you. Because of this, your present behavior and attitudes may be very disconnected from the true you. Remember how boring it is to live disconnected from your true self compared to when you were a free and easy child.

When you carry around a huge sub-conscious catalogue of memories designed to determine every one of your actions, your life becomes one monotonous re-run after the next.

If you're just doing what you always do – that's because it's what you're programmed to do. You've been programmed by your parents, your culture and the people who've had power over you when you were young.

Imagine this: You are met with the opportunity to do something amazingly spontaneous and impulsive. You get that feeling in your gut, like you're about to jump out of an airplane, when you consider following this powerful impulse. It's outrageous and it's totally you.

What if you refuse this call? Your mind floods with imagery of all sorts of failure, retribution, shame, guilt and heartache that you might associate with taking this kind of impulsive risk.

Do you know where all that trepidation came from? When you were a young child, you depended on adults for your survival. Chances are these adults weren't completely aware of the amazing beauty that you just had naturally. You were spontaneously beautiful and sincere because you were un-adult-erated.

Because you're a DaVinci you were probably pretty impulsive as a child. Chances are most adults weren't appreciative of your unexpected impulsive moves. Your impulses led you to do things that were threatening to their sense of control.

Your pure unadulterated impulses, full of spontaneous wisdom, most likely violated the limited beliefs and expectations of the adults around you. I believe your purest impulses come from wisdom far wiser than the human intellect. I believe they stem from the collective unconscious, which always knows more than we do and initiates these impulses with the greater good in mind.

Your impulsive expressions would probably wreak havoc on the plans of your caretakers, but who says their plans were good ones? You have been punished many times for being transcendently right; doing what no one knew at the time had to be done. You may have saved your community years of trouble with one little catastrophe you made that distracted them from making a bigger one; but nonetheless you were likely the one to get punished for your service.

Remember the old adage:
"A good deed never goes unpunished."

The adult figures of your childhood had no idea what they were doing when they abused your delicate system of miraculous impulses. They had no idea how incredibly right you were. They had no idea of the miracles you shed with every little release of impulsive genius, because it was so far beyond their comprehension that they probably squashed it out of fear and ignorance and maybe unconscious jealousy at your brilliance. Your brilliance betrayed their egocentric control and mediocrity.

What egos do to suppress God's wisdom is punish those who become His messengers. You were His messenger and so you were punished ceaselessly until, maybe you no longer chose to be His messenger again.

Punishment and severe reprimands are designed to break the Spirit. They are designed to shock the recipient in order to embed negative associations with whatever was just expressed. That negative association is often stored in your memory as eidetic imagery. It now serves the purpose of influencing your subconscious choices around that kind of expression. Think of this psychic imagery as bricks in a wall between you and your truest will.

At first, the bricks seem to merely act as deterrents against you being so spontaneous and free. In the beginning of this indoctrination you can still see beyond these bricks in order to still occasionally express your true will. But that negative imagery keeps being built up reprimand after reprimand until you are no longer free; until you are no longer you.

Eventually these bricks can pile up so high that they cast a long shadow over the landscape of your soul. You may forget what it ever was you truly wanted and you may become a slave to society's rules.

This wall stands as a warning against being too free and honoring your genuine will. It sets up a conflict in you. Will you choose to heed the wall and only do what the world has told you to – or will you go ahead and fearlessly do what your soul whispers is it's truest desire for you this very moment?

If your mom or dad was here right now, realizing what they had done, you know they would probably be deeply saddened by it. They might say something like, "I had no idea the incredible beauty you were offering us. I never meant to cause this shame. I only hope you can find your true will again."

So hold no grudges, because that is not your path to healing. Your parents did the best they could. Now it is your turn to take your progression and healing to the next level.

When you start choosing your own will, it is likely you will go through a period of deep confusion. You will notice your spontaneous impulses leading you to work little miracles throughout your day. But you may also find it difficult to navigate your life without the opinions of others steering you. Now it is time for your inner wisdom to become your guide; and that can take some getting used to.

The key here is to learn to remember what it is you are here for. Your genuine soulful impulses will show you the way. But that wall may loom large and behind that wall is everything you forgot you forgot.

Remembering what you forgot you forgot

Have you ever have run upstairs to get something and then found yourself there, and had to ask yourself "what am I doing here?' Ever watch previews and forget what movie you were there to see? This is the story of your life if you don't listen to your soul.

What are you conscious of?

"Should you read this chapter, or the next?" "Should you subscribe to cable, or DSL?" "Should you watch Jay Leno, or David Letterman?" "Do you *really want* to super-size that?" These are not real choices, they are distractions. They pull you away from your deeper choice. They drag you into a trance of information overload. They seduce you away from your true relationships with others.

These decisions steal what little room for intimacy you still have left in your busy life.

You may be tempted to steal a moment that you could have shared with someone you love; but instead you exchange it for something else. You might use that moment to read a senseless trade journal article, watch another TV show, download another piece of useless Internet data; all in the hopes that this new media will somehow save you from yourself. The endless sea of information keeps pulling you deeper and deeper until it overwhelms you. Your mind begins to race. Frantically you will throw good time after bad, hoping you will not drown before you are vindicated from this careless dive.

Although you see yourself making decision after decision, they all lead to nothing, to nowhere, just deeper into the hole. No more input will save you now. No clever decision will set you free. You have forgotten something far more important.

For, it was not information, but devotion that could have saved you all along.

You see, we can be entrenched in a Pavlovian script of stimulus-response decision making. We can experience ourselves as no more than emotional droids. We can lose consciousness of our very being and aliveness. It is then that we are unaware of the greater choice, dangling high from the heavens, reaching down to touch us, just above our heads. All we need to do is look up from our tasks and we will see it once again.

Because we are human, we long for more. We feel a calling to a greater experience, but often we just don't remember where to look.

Sometimes when I go to a movie, I am overwhelmed by the coming attractions. I become so captivated by the dazzling imagery, sounds and stories that I actually forget which movie it was that I was coming to see. Then I wonder, "If, in just ten minutes, it is so easy to forget the entire purpose of my movie-going adventure, then how easy must it be to forget, over many, many years, the entire purpose of my life?"

It is not just that we forget why we came, it is even worse. We forget that we have forgotten why we came. We don't even have the memory of a memory to wonder about.

Living consciously is remembering constantly. It is imperative, for if at any moment we forget, we may not remember again for a long long time. We will not even realize that we have forgotten, because we will also have forgotten that we have forgotten.

So easy is it to forget. So slippery and subtle is the slope down into the trance of living unconsciously. And how can we know, for every slip from consciousness becomes, by definition, unconscious.

When we are nodding off, falling back into that helpless trance, let us kindly nudge each other awake. Let us show one another that there is always further to go, still higher to lift. Let us help carry each other through those vulnerable times, when tears are all that can be mustered; because on the other side of those tears is where freedom is found. Without love to remind us of our mission, it is far too easy to forget, to drift off … and to slide back down, down into another daydream, down into that pitiful trance; and this time, the trance may last our entire lifetime.

However, if instead of daydreaming about what we should do tomorrow, we realize this opportunity to choose how we will look upon "right now". This is the greater choice, and then we are free. Instantly, on that pivot of choice, our whole consciousness swings. We are more skillful and awake. Our vision is clear. Our eyes are bright with anticipation. Our old and dreary world has become new again. Suddenly, we experience the wild expansive freedom of living consciously. This is the ultimate rush.

Let your consciousness regain its natural buoyancy. Let your consciousness float high above the chaos to a place where simple acts of kindness, healing and sharing become the natural focus.

There *is* a place like that, you know. All you must do is put yourself there.

The Visionary Power Cycle

"You may insist that the God does not answer
you, but it might be wiser to consider the kind of
questioner you are.
You do not ask only for what you want.
This is because you are afraid you might receive it,
and you would."

~ A Course in Miracles

Begin with a Prayer. Ask God "What is the most helpful question I can ask?" then wait and listen. Listen with the intent of receiving an answer, but don't jump to conclusions about what that answer is. Just be still and quiet as long as you feel is comfortable, then continue for a minute or two more – your first hint will come then – right after the discomfort subsides.

Dream and image stream holding the intention to have your question answered. What are the clues you are given? What way are you feeling is the way to go now? Are you being honest? Do you feel joy and peace when you consider this new direction? Once you feel that you have a genuine direction to proceed with, start the next step.

Visualize yourself succeeding in this new direction. Anchor this vision of success in your mind. Ride this visualization like a Disney ride again and again. When you are doing this well, you will begin to actually *feel* what it will be like when you succeed. Keep reinforcing these positive feelings with your visualizations. It is the feelings that will help you find your way there.

Because you are an eidetic imager, your visualizations are vast and immersive. They feel life-like and real – especially to your subconscious. Your eidetic visualizations will program your subconscious to help you attract the experiences you are visualizing.

You might ask "If visualizing is so powerful, why doesn't everybody do it?" A big part of the answer to that is, 9 out of 10 are not eidetic imagers, so visualizing isn't as powerful for them as it is for DaVincis.

Some of the best Olympic athletes use visualization to help them win their way to gold medals – most great athletes are DaVincis. As part of their training, they visualize themselves performing perfectly and winning. If you're an eidetic imager, your visualizations can be quite powerful and should work especially well for you.

You must be careful with visualization. It can be like a genie in a bottle. Often ego-driven wishes combined with powerful visualization can backfire and cause more suffering.

Learn the simple secret to mastering a holy form of visualization that will only bring you closer to heaven and help you avoid unnecessary suffering in your life. It's powerful and real …

You will find it here: **www.DaVinciMethod.com/visualize**

The DaVinci Day

"A well-spent day brings happy sleep"

~ Leonardo da Vinci

Begin your day, right when you begin to wake up, by recounting your night's dreams and imagery. Do your best to make these images "stick" in your conscious mind while you are still half-way between conscious and unconscious. Once you feel you have retrieved as much of your night's unconscious sounds, feelings and imagery as your conscious mind can handle, go ahead and become alert enough to record them somehow. I find an audio-recorder or a pen and paper work well for this. Later in your day when you are fully alert you can refer back to these notes to discover what gems await you in them.

Now that you have adequately recorded whatever gifts received during the night from your powerful and brilliant unconscious mind, visualize the kind of day you would like to have.

Now say to yourself "I can have this beautiful day that I want if I make no decisions by myself." Then surrender the guidance for your day to God. Your higher self will retain this invitation and will begin receiving the divine inspiration that will serve as an answer to your silent prayer for your day's unfoldment.

Start the day with completing your most important and difficult goal for the day. After that everything else becomes free and easy.

At the end of your work day figure out what you would like to accomplish tomorrow and establish a clear vision of that.

At night program your unconscious to bring your aspirations to life:

"I have discovered that it is of some use that when you lie in bed at night, and gaze into the darkness, to repeat in your mind the things you have been studying. Not only does it help the understanding, but also the memory."

~ Leonardo da Vinci

The DaVinci Method Daily Regime

The DaVinci Method includes a daily regime. This regime is an acknowledgment of your genetic needs. The first part of this regime is physical. It's an acknowledgment of your physical genetic needs – your DRD4 gene. One of those genetic needs is a high level of intense exercise, so you want to get 45 minutes to an hour of intense exercise every day and that's best done in the beginning of your day.

If you lift weights, you can do bursts of weight lifting, and you can do circuit training at the gym, and that can be pretty intense. But what we DaVinci types enjoy most is sports and activities where you get to play. Part of having the DaVinci trait is being a great intuitive player, you know, really enjoying play and making some great spontaneous moves. Play helps you get out of yourself more and get more into your flow. Any kind of athletic activity that lets you play is great. It can be spontaneous, or have a powerful flow; but whatever it is, let it be enlivening.

Choose something that's your style. Most likely that's highly engaged sports like touch football, soccer, squash or tennis – anything that involves lots room for spontaneous brilliance and short bursts of intense activity are great things for you.

Also, kick boxing classes aren't bad because if they have energizing music and choreography, they have flow and also offer short bursts of intense activity. So, if you're not competitive and you prefer to be in an aerobics room, kick boxing, martial arts, and dancing types of activities could be good. In fact, you want to look for any activity where you're really sweating and getting those short sprint-like bursts of activity.

That's Step One. You've got to have your exercise down, and you've got to do it three to six times a week.

This is often easier said than done. It can become really difficult to get back into the high levels of athletic prowess available to the DaVinci because the longer you deny your natural state the more likely you will be repulsed by the very activity that is best for you. If you don't do what's best for you, you regret it; and that regret can fester and make you feel guilty and angry.

When you finally get around to getting back into physical fitness, you may find you have a lot of anger at this idea that somehow you are being forced or coerced into having to work out. But what you're really mad about is that you let yourself get out of shape, that you let your identification slip from being an athlete to being a couch potato. Now you might see getting back into shape as a form of admitting that you were wrong.

Forget all that! Forgive yourself for judging yourself for not getting much exercise the last couple decades. There's still time.

But now's the time; because you really do need a lot of exercise – much more than 9 out of 10 people you know. It's your genetic make-up that wants intense activity almost every day, and you can't escape your genetic make-up – at least in this lifetime. The trick is to do it, to dread it, but do it, and keep doing it. Eventually it will become a habit. Dread and do.

Dread and do.

Dread and do. At first the dread can be big and the do small; but eventually the dread becomes tiny, because what you can do is huge.

This is one aspect of the DaVinci Method regime.

Then go for a 20 minute walk in the afternoon to clear your head. If you bring a good listener you can use this time to clear your head. If you bring a friend this is a good time for deepening your relationship. I used to take long walks with my father. It was very healing.

Creativity

"Talent may be in time forgiven,
but genius never"

~ Lord Byron

The second aspect is you've got to devote an hour a day to some sort of creative endeavor – and we're going to put some guidelines on what creative means. Creativity means "from the inside out." Not outside in. You're not to just regurgitate what you've been taught or what you've consumed. Genuine creativity is not a reflection of good consumption; it's a reflection of genuine honesty leading to moments of inspiration.

So, this time is not about taking other people's ideas and making them your own. It's much more honest and pure. Creativity is using honest self expression to clear a channel for greatness to come through you. Then it's no longer you, it's the Creator working through you. You are just an honest conduit. Leonardo DaVinci could be incredibly honest.

This is your creative time. This is not time to be developing a skill. This is not a time where you are trying to abide by external rules, external guidelines, or trying to develop an external habit. Even something that seems like it's creative, such as painting or drawing or music – if you're just learning to play the piano and you have to do drills and exercises to develop the skill of playing the piano, that's not creative. That's just developing a skill. When you finally have enough skill to honestly express and play on the piano the music the Creator is whispering in your ear, then that's creative.

If you want to draw and you're taking drawing classes to learn the skills of drawing, that's not creative – that's also learning a skill. That can be good to participate in though, because the more skills you know, the more rewarding your creative time can be. However, remember you're using this time to take what's inside of *you* and draw it out of *you,* not copy something outside of you to perfection.

Free writing is great. Journaling is great. You just write. You've got to just write – you don't write for your writing to be shown off or to have anyone ever read. That's exhibitionistic not creative. Just keep writing privately for you.

You don't have to be good at using the particular instruments you choose for your creative time – be it the piano, a pen, or watercolors; pottery, your voice or your body in dance. You can be downright unskillful with your instrument of choice, but as long as you find something you can truly lose yourself in, then you've won.

Now do it for a half-an-hour to an hour every day.

What is journaling?

Journaling is just sitting down with a pad of paper and writing out everything that flies through your consciousness. It's also called train of consciousness.

If nothing comes to your mind, you write – "nothing's coming to my mind right now. I can't think of anything – this is boring. I don't know what I'm doing here. I'm feeling crazy. Why do I feel so crazy? Maybe it's because of that guy, the other day, that said those mean words to me, I wish I had something smart to say back at him, my boss is a jerk, but I really like that girl who is the receptionist." Whatever. You just write anything. Let out all your really dark, deep secrets that you keep hidden even from yourself. It's okay here, because you're going to burn it all afterwards. Write them out, and then burn it afterwards.

This is never for someone to read. You have to have integrity about your process, which means if you're free writing, and you say to yourself, "I can write about anything, because I will keep this writing sacred," and you can trust yourself, a lot of crap and a lot of brilliance will come through.

Now, you can – if you reach a point where you're really writing well, and you don't have to worry about having writer's block or not having good, rich material, you can say to yourself, "Okay, this time I'm going to write for a half an hour or an hour, and I may want to show this off sometime."

I recommend you only do that after you've really developed a habit of writing honestly, after you've done a number of days of successful writing, where you really feel like you've gotten a lot out, meaning that a lot of the subconscious or unconscious things inside of you have come out in your writing, and you've gained in awareness, and you really feel like you've purged, and now you recognize "Now I'm starting to write well, maybe tomorrow I'll share what I've written."

Train of consciousness doesn't have to be limited to writing. It can be singing. It can be drawing or doodling. It can be anything that just lets you pull from within and bring it out. It can be dancing even. It can be anything that is full of expression and spontaneous. You just need to express yourself for a good half an hour to an hour every day. You need to make a safe environment for your muse to be free.

Transcending Addiction

What if anything done compulsively, was the result of repeatedly sublimating our true impulses?

Because impulsive expression is so often regarded as "unacceptable" by our culture, us impulsive DaVinci types have been thoroughly trained to distrust and sublimate our frequent impulses. So in order to "control" our impulses maybe we develop culturally acceptable channels to release this libido energy for each impulse.

Maybe it's eating, maybe it's smoking, maybe it's drinking, maybe it's working, maybe exercise. Whatever it is, it's probably something much more contained and controlled than expressing a spontaneous impulse - like kissing a stranger.

While our spontaneous impulses may be disruptive - they are also healthy.

Unfortunately, when we begin to consciously force the release of that impulsive libido energy into the same controlled, predictable action again and again, that action quickly becomes habitual. Although ultimately self-destructive this compulsive libido sublimation feels safer than the honest expression of our many unique, unpredictable (and often socially dangerous) spontaneous impulses.

It's high time for us DaVincis to let those true spontaneous impulses express through us honestly. Hug your neighbor, ask that stranger out, don't be afraid to shout. It's far better than becoming a burn-out.

"Cowardice" – A Story of Addiction

Once there was a cowardly man who knew nothing of his true Self. He cowered in fear, he robbed, and stole, cheated and lied his way through life. He had no friends, except for those who he felt he could gain materially from, but they were not "real friends" in his mind, they were "assets." This cowardly man did not trust life further than he could throw it; and more than that, he could not even trust himself. He wanted control instead of trust and at every pass he found ways to take control away from the trusting.

This man was sad and very lonely and he turned to bad habits to ease his pain. He drank, and he womanized; he binged and he smoked; he was compulsive and abusive with himself and others.

This cowardly man started becoming fat and old ahead of his time. Each day felt more like hell than the last. "What is happening to me?" he thought. He was so good at stealing control, but now he could hardly control himself. Every morning, after a night of binge drinking, binge eating, binge smoking, or binge sex, he would wake up angry at himself. Each morning he would say "That's it, I'm going to get control of my life today." Only he would repeat the whole sad episode all over again that night.

Something was wrong. As much as he wanted to stop his bad habits, there was some irresistible force inside him that would build and build and build until he crumbled under its magnitude and went for that "fix" to relieve the pressure. Some days it was gambling, other days it was stuffing himself with food, or wasting hours downloading Internet porn. Finally there were days when all he could do was get loaded and pass out to escape the torture of his own mind.

He felt desperate.

That is, until one day, he made an amazing discovery. He didn't need to stop it. This force that would build inside him, overpowering him and compelling him to compulsive behavior and self abuse, was actually a good thing. He had just not channeled it correctly.

This irresistible force had the power to work miracles. Instead of trying to control it, subvert it, sublimate it, second guess it, suppress it or fight it, he could just allow the force to spontaneously work through him. When he let the force work through him, the moment he felt that tingle of anticipation, it would spontaneously push him to do the most miraculous things.

DaVinci Addiction Therapy

"Recent investigations have found that up to 50%
of individuals with continuing ADHD symptoms
have a substance-use disorder.
ADHD appears to represent an independent risk
factor for substance abuse."

~ ANNALS OF THE NEW YORK ACADEMY
OF SCIENCES (June 1, 2001)

Right now, as you think of your addiction, I'll bet you have many powerful and conflicting feelings washing over you in succession. Waves of longing. Waves of guilt. Waves of regret. Waves of compulsion. Waves of denial. Waves of anxiety. Waves of depression.

We are not victims of these feelings. We *are* in charge, once we accept help. The help is an invincible force within us, which once we learn to work with it, will not only help us hold these waves back, but will realign our energies to be used constructively.

Addiction is the misinterpretation of subconscious impulses, acted upon and reinforced with guilt (self-hatred). It is a massive waste of time. It is also an attempt to attack ourselves, and those around us, by withholding the greatest gifts we can offer.

Those of us with addictive tendencies possess a huge potential. We have managed to repress a good deal less of our own impulsive nature. Ordinarily the lack of "adequate" levels of repression is met with much cultural reprimand. This potential is so powerful, that if it is not expressed it becomes quite a burden. It is also so powerful that when it is expressed, it can obliterate sorrow, pain and entire chunks of the space-time continuum. Let me explain.

There is a theory that, at every moment, we are offered heaven-on-earth (perfect peace and joy), but we consistently refuse it. So, space-time exists to give us the time and space to experience the intolerable pain of not accepting peace and joy, allowing us to finally realize that we do in fact want to accept everlasting peace and joy.

And when we do, we are finally free.

Until then we get to experience every form and degree of pain we wish. We can get really down and dirty. We get to roll around in it and wallow in it. Then one day, we hit our threshold for pain and we start to look for another way. This book is (hopefully) about the other way.

The other way is always there, waiting for us. It is a constant impulse that builds in us until we express it or sublimate it. When we express it, we are overwhelmed with joy. When we sublimate it, we feel great discomfort until it is expressed later, usually in a destructive way. It is the miracle-impulse.

Us folks with addictive or extreme behavior could be said to have very strong miracle-impulses. When we don't express these impulses they get bottled up inside and make us really uncomfortable. We feel itchy, scratchy, like we're going to jump out of our skin. (Our ego is based on our skin so we're really preparing to jump out of our egos!) Now, we have a choice. Do we have the courage to allow the miracle-impulse to express *itself?* Or do we sublimate it into a more "controlled" expression of our conscious choosing?

Most of us have learned to sublimate our miracle impulses from a very young age. Our parents just didn't understand and couldn't handle just how right we were when we would let those miracles rip as kids. So we learned to repress our miracle-impulse. But a subconscious impulse cannot be fully repressed; it will get out in one form or another.

You know that feeling just keeps building until you can't repress it anymore. It's no use fighting yourself. You just can't win. When you are your own opponent, you must also lose.

Our egos want control, so they continue to try to reroute all of our explosive impulses into one "controlled" and "predictable" expression. Unfortunately, that expression may have seemed more culturally appropriate in the beginning phase of this rerouting process; once a critical mass of impulses are being rerouted into the same compulsive expression channel the frequency of this kind of expression becomes EXTREME. It has become addictive behavior.

The solution?

Repress the addictive behavior? C'mon we know that doesn't really work. We can't deny it. Ever noticed how many "recovering addicts," of other behaviors pick up smoking as they try to sublimate their old addiction? This is just another rerouting. We're trying to solve the problem with the same kind of thinking that made it in the first place.

Many of us have heard of the sexual-impulse or the fight-or-flight-impulse, but most of us have not considered the miracle-impulse. You see the miracle-impulse is the king of all impulses. It is the strongest impulse we have and yet we don't even know it's at work because we have put so much effort into suppressing it's expression!

Here's why: Expressing a miracle-impulse is seen as very dangerous to our ego. Miracle-impulses, if allowed to express themselves, can seem quite embarrassing. That is because we don't know where they come from. They inspire words and actions, which our conscious mind does not understand. We fear what we do not understand, thus if we are attempting to consciously direct the miracle-impulse we will become afraid. This is why we must surrender to the miracle-impulse and allow It to work us. We feel responsible for its expression, but we're not. It is a higher power at work through us. A power that we have learned to deny is inside us.

So, for addiction therapy, add more of what you want – attempting to merely take away what you're hooked on will leave you feeling empty, vacant and terrified – but instead crowding out the undesirable with the good will make you feel full and content. The good will eventually become a habit and it will take over any remembered glimmer of craving for your old addictions.

A Story of Two Dogs

One morning after a restless night

I approached my spiritual master

And confessed,

"Master, it is like there are two dogs

Battling for command of my heart

One dog represents the yearnings of my Soul

The other dog represents the yearnings of my flesh,

These two dogs are strong,

and the battle that rages in my heart is fierce.

I am afraid the battle could go either way.

Tell me master, how can I know which dog will win?"

The master calmly smiled,

with a twinkling of recognition in his eyes,

he said, "You can know, because the dog that will win …

… is the dog that you feed."

Where is the "Method" already?!

Some of you may wonder, "Where's the method?" This *is* The DaVinci *Method* after all. The answer is, the absence of method *is* the Method. It is the relinquishment of all methods that leads a DaVinci into their brilliance. The DaVinci Method is the urgent imperative, "Know thyself." For only self-knowledge can liberate a DaVinci to discover their brilliance and their greatness.

Methods are inherently outside of you. They are the external rules that most Normal types worship. DaVinci types, however, become corrupted by external rules when they worship them like idols. Methods inherently contain "shoulds," directions or rules that too often become false gods. DaVincis have an inner guidance system that is far superior to any outer directive; and the key to following that guidance is to surrender the feeling of needing any outer frameworks, systems, laws, rules or methods to tell you what to do.

Methods are those things you have been taught all your life to honor more than your very own heart and soul. What confusion and disconnection you have suffered because of that! The person on the brink of suicide is often cornered by "shoulds," which they believe, cherish and honor over the callings and needs of their own heart, to the point that they feel the need to kill themselves to escape.

The DaVinci Method is an anti-method. It is the one method that will help you shed all the limitations that have been placed on you, believing you needed to follow someone else's way instead of having faith in your own infinitely intelligent inner Guidance.

Anything linear, fully comprehensible, and "set in stone" will only inhibit you and make you more neurotic, especially if you ritualize it. Civilization is based on trying to set things in stone. Look at all the rules, laws, and stone structures civilization has built. These things, over thousands of years of civilization, have not overcome the most basic of human tragedies. Society cannot save you. It can only exploit you and further its own mindless agenda. It is as sure to fail you as it has failed the rest of the world throughout time.

You have been indoctrinated to honor the fundamental prerequisite of civilization: "Follow our rules and you'll be safe." You have been punished again and again until you accepted that rules carry with them greater authority than your own inner knowing.

"Then the worst thing happened that could happen to any fighter ... he got civilized."

~ "Mick" in Rocky III

So why do you seek and accept outer directives for your own life? Because you are afraid of the answers you will find in your heart. Because you have been told all your life that your heart will get you into trouble; and it *will*. But the kind of trouble that your heart will get you into is the sweetest trouble you will ever have. It is the juice of life. It is the wild girlfriends or boyfriends, the crazy jobs, the impractical pursuits, the unplanned adventures, the unexpected babies. It is all the choices that "should" have resulted in disaster, but somehow became the greatest events of your life. That is where your heart is leading you. That is where no method ever can.

Your heart will lead you on wild journeys where you will experience life to its fullest. You may not have a perfectly balanced checking account. You may not always be able to find your keys. But when you are following your heart none of it will matter so much. Your keys might be lost, but you will have found your own soul. You will feel alive and vibrant and you will be doing the *good* work. Your life will become the great adventure that movies are made of, and you will finally be the hero.

Do you still want a method? **Here's your method:**

Every day, let yourself become a little more free. Every day follow your deepest impulses a bit more heartily. Every day spend more time following your heart and less time bowing to the rules in your head. Every day become more relentlessly honest with yourself and others. Every day do something so spontaneous that it makes you feel truly alive. Your spontaneous impulses, your connection to Guidance, your unfettered trust in your own impeccable instincts; that shall be your "method".

So now you can say there is method to your madness. But you and I both know that the ideal is **no method**; there is simply genius behind your madness, and you are finally recognizing it. You are tapped into the Divine Order; and you are finally realizing that the resultant "madness" you express might be a good thing.

> *"In a world full of people, only some want to fly –*
> *isn't that crazy? ... You know we're never going*
> *to survive – unless we get a little crazy."*
>
> ~ Seal

Methods are like software CDs for your brain. While the software is still only on the CD, and thus external to the computer, it is slow for it to load. Similarly while you operate by methods that are outside of you, your actions will be slow and forced as opposed to spontaneous and free. The ideal is to take an outer method that seems attractive, discover the underlying principles that make it work, and install the underlying principles into your consciousness. Then you are not "acting" according to the tyranny of outer rules; but instead you are powerfully "being" in spontaneity and freedom with the guidance of well chosen inner principles. My son, John once said to me, "I don't even need the CD in my computer. I just go there right away ... I used to need the CD, but now I don't." When you let go of methods and rules and trust your inner guidance, you can "just go there right away." Instead of stumbling over decisions, trying to play by man-made rules, you only need follow one rule, your heart's.

That is how you will be once you get the hang of living your life freely, honestly, spontaneously. At first you'll have to remind yourself that it's okay to just be you in every moment, and do whatever you feel like doing. But soon you'll see how powerfully positive and productive the real you is when you just let yourself be. You'll learn to trust that the impulses of your heart are for the highest good, no matter how much trouble they may seem to cause.

Now you can release yourself from all you thought you were and become what you truly are. What keeps you bound in chains other than your own beliefs about what how you "should" be?

Sometimes it seems as if we'd rather fail, than succeed. We'd rather be small and unnoticed than be large and a target. We'd rather pretend to be weak than be seen as strong.

So much of life is wasted, seeking without finding, trying without actually doing, just going through the motions trying to look like you're following the rules. You could be following your own heart instead and then everything you do is a victory. When you follow outer directives, there is always someone else to blame for your failure. But when you shed all that, you have no one to blame your failure on. No one to say to, "See? Look what you made me do." You become 100% responsible and 100% response able. You are finally empowered to live your own life to the fullest.

Let yourself experience that uneasy feeling of realizing your vast power and becoming aware of how much life you've wasted just pretending to be small. On the other side of that grief is the freedom to really enjoy the rest of your life.

Feigning weakness often feels cozy and familiar. It wraps a blanket of limitations around your life and keeps you "safe" in your place. On the other hand, to claim your strength is to throw that warm blanket aside; and realize and breathe in the invigorating air of the spacious world of opportunities. This world is subtly offered to you everyday. Limitlessness is exhilarating! You are powerful indeed when you truly come alive.

To cling to a single method to unlock your brilliance is to limit the very expression of your limitless brilliance. The neurotic limitation of your expression is to deny the spontaneous creative brilliance that is yours, in order to adhere to some antiquated "should" that you learned. The very reason you have needed to read this book instead of just going out into the vast and breathtaking world and reveling in your own power and majesty, is that you believed that you needed to be told how to live. The truth is that you already know how, you just need to trust yourself.

> *"Whoever says to this mountain, `Be removed and be cast into the sea,' and does not doubt in his heart, but believes that those things he says will be done, he will have whatever he says. Therefore I say to you, whatever things you ask when you pray, believe that you receive them, and you will have them."*

> ~ Jesus Christ – Mark 11:22-24

Believe in your God given power! You have it. All you've got to do is trust it. Trust your heart. Trust your deepest impulses. Trust Life.

Still don't believe me? Watch this 60 second clip and ask yourself "Do any of these great DaVincis appear to follow an outer method?" Watch it here: **www.DaVinciMethod.com/CrazyOnes**

Surrendering to the Miracle-Impulse

There are three aspects of the surrender required when expressing a miracle-impulse.

Surrender to the awareness that you are in fact experiencing the call of a miracle-impulse. Surrender to your heart's control of the expression of this miracle-impulse. (Without your heart's wisdom and guidance many miracle-impulses can become misfires, depleting and confusing you.)

Surrender to the person you are called upon to express your miracle-impulse with. This may involve a major act of forgiveness on your part. The level of intimacy and trust required may be quite uncomfortable for you. You must relax your inhibitions and allow yourself the time and space to express your miracle-impulse the way you are inwardly guided to.

Forgive any self-judgments you may try to lay upon your own behavior or worthiness of this miracle. Recognize that fear or shame of an expressed miracle-impulse is simply due to your inherent lack of understanding of what a miracle really is and who you really are.

Common and clear examples of miracle-impulses being expressed occur in acts of childbirth. Childbirth has been said by many mothers to be "faith renewing." You will eventually note that all miracles, when expressed, are faith renewing.

When discerning if an impulse you feel is truly a miracle-impulse to be surrendered to – trust your heart.

Trust your heart – because your heart knows the truth. Your heart can tell truth from falsehood. Your heart can guide you to honesty and offer you the deepest most powerful answers – if only you'll ask and listen.

We've gotten so used to bowing to "expert opinions" that we've forsaken the opinions of our own hearts. That's how we've been led so far astray.

The only reliable expert is in your heart. Margaret Mead said, "Art is the language that is the language of the heart". Start listening to it and heed what your heart tells you.

That's what being the Artist is all about! That's the way it works.

God speaks through your heart.

The DaVinci Knighthood

I think when I say this, I may speak for a generation. When I was a child, I wanted to be a Jedi Knight from George Lucas's epic tale, Star Wars. Sure it was just a great story, but something rang true about it. The Jedi Knight was a symbol of something far more profound and archetypal than just a movie character.

What has become clear is that the hero's journey – a mythological story template that many great movies are based on – is a system of guideposts for a great DaVinci life.

The Hero's Journey is a story template discovered by Joseph Campbell that is at the heart of almost every great mythological story of heroism throughout the history of mankind.

Mythology can tell us secrets about the deeper nature of things. They have been refined over hundreds of years through the crucible of retelling. When something in a mythological story rang true, it stayed in the tale to be retold to others. If something in the story did not ring true it tended to be forgotten in the retelling. When a story stays circulating long enough it is refined to the point that it becomes a myth. A myth is a story that clearly conveys the underlying ineffable truth of the human experience.

If you look at the many Hero's Journeys used in cinema and stories you will note that all of the heroes are classic DaVinci types.

Luke in Star Wars can't be a simple farmer on an isolated planet, like his aunt and uncle insist he should be. He needs to be right where the action is and so, in true DaVinci form, he joins the Rebels against the Evil Empire.

In another classic Hero's Journey based movie, The Matrix, Neo can't be content as an anonymous software programmer working in a cubicle for an oppressive corporation. So he takes the red pill from his rebel computer hacker mentor, because he has to know the truth of his existence. He longs in his heart for the Great Adventure.

Something calls to us from these stories, because we recognize ourselves in these heroes. We DaVincis need the Great Adventure to feel truly alive.

The Hero's Journey seems to be a hidden message for all us DaVinci types that there is an alternative to spending the rest of your life in a cubicle.

There is a saying that "The unexamined life is not worth living." This may be true, but even more relevant to DaVinci types is the retort that "The un-lived life is not worth examining."

The Hero's Journey calls us to live our lives in a remarkable way. To live fearlessly, to battle the false gods of our lives and our cultures, to surrender to the kind of struggle that turns mere mortals white with trepidation.

You as a DaVinci were put here to *live* the Hero's Journey – not just watch it on TV. When you are not "on your journey" you have that familiar sinking feeling that your life is being wasted.

Luckily today we have an analysis of the archetypal Hero's Journey that offers a road map, showing you where you are and where you are going in relation to this predestined journey that you can no longer deny.

I hate to break it you, but as a DaVinci your life will be a struggle. All heroes struggle. It can be a gloriously good struggle if you surrender to your journey, but it will be a struggle nonetheless.

Either you struggle, as you must, while you press forward through your own Hero's Journey; or struggle with all of the vices, addictions, depression and disorders that befall a DaVinci who is Refusing the Call.

Sensitivity to the ring of truth and trusting your heart will be an imperative on your Hero's Journey. Let go of your conscious self. Let your feelings guide you now.

> *"There is something in every one of you that waits*
> *and listens for the sound of the genuine in*
> *yourself. It is the only true guide you will ever*
> *have. And if you cannot hear it, you will all of*
> *your life spend your days on the ends of strings*
> *that somebody else pulls."*
> ~ Howard Thurman

If you go online to **www.DaVinciMethod.com/hero** you will find an outline of the archetypal Hero's Journey by which you can navigate your new life.

How did you succeed? ... "I had to."

> *"Geniuses are the luckiest of mortals*
> *because what they must do is the same as*
> *what they most want to do."*
>
> ~ W. H. Auden

Once you are on your hero's journey, I'm sorry to say, you can't go back. You can never go back. Your life will never work again the old way, because you no longer will fit in that small place that you were once squeezed into.

And it's not just that you won't fit back in your old life and your old ways – there's something even more mysterious and more powerful that will stop you if you try.

If you begin your hero's journey and then decide to quit and go back to your old way of life, all of the doors that you once opened easily will close in your face. You won't be able to get the same kind of jobs you easily won and faked before. You won't be able to get your way with the same tricks that used to work so easily before, because now they've lost their magic. Your tricks lose their magic when you're no longer self-deceived and you don't believe your own B.S. anymore. Everything that was once easy for you to fake, will become hard if not impossible. When you have changed, the sad place you once called home will no longer let you in.

This is the "tough love" side of God and the invisible hands that shape your life. This is the power of your unconscious mind to overwhelm your silly little schemes to try to escape your destiny. This is the giant and powerful unconscious mind subtly but powerfully forcing your hand towards what it knows is best for you. Or, if you are more spiritually minded, you might enjoy seeing this as some amazing divine force moving you forward along your path, not allowing you to stray.

When you are too neurotic and have neutralized your own will, your unconscious mind will find ways to make fate force your hand. This allows you to take the necessary steps on your journey while alleviating the guilt of being different from what you were taught you should be. "Divine intervention," "Angelic assistance" and "Invisible hands" are positive expressions of this phenomenon.

Often if you listen to great artists when they are asked, "How did you do it?" they answer something like, "I never gave up. It was very difficult. I suffered a lot. But I just had to do it."

"Genius is perseverance in disguise"

~ Mike Newlin

The key here is that the artist is revealing, "I had to do it." I used to think this meant something like, "I was single mindedly bent on doing it." And to some degree it does. But after traveling a ways along my own journey, I have discovered something deeper about that statement.

One morning after suffering another devastating blow to my ego in my attempts to return back to the fake but comfortable way of life I once had, I realized that I no longer had much choice about my own career. I couldn't take my old career back – there was always what felt like some supernatural force that would stop me at every turn. All sorts of things beyond my control would rush in to stop me from retreating to my old life. It was so blatant at times that it became painfully comical.

I realized that with regard to doing the work I was called to do, I no longer could avoid doing it – at least without experiencing significant penalties. As far as doing what I was being led to do, "I just had to do it" or I would continue to suffer a relentless parade of unexplainable setbacks and frustrations. There was no way out of it: To continue to resist my destiny meant I would have constant frustration. To accept the journey to my destiny, (as scary as it seemed), meant maybe one day, with enough humility and patience, I could actually succeed again. The great news is that new success would not be with some goal or career that my heart was not really into, it would be a success for my very soul.

So, when an accomplished DaVinci says they, "just had to do it", what they are revealing is a subtle but extraordinarily powerful aspect of commitment to one's truth. When you finally allow your heart and soul to commit to your true purpose, there is no stopping you. Not even you can really stop you anymore. You can kick and scream and tantrum and delay, but somehow that greater part of you keeps raising the stakes until you finally give up and do what you've always deeply wanted to do.

The same experience is likely to become evident in your life as you accept your own Hero's Journey in becoming a relentlessly creative DaVinci. Don't seek your old comforts, because their appeal will evaporate in the heat of your newfound passions. Don't cling to your old ideas of safety, because those illusions of protection will dissolve in the light of your newfound strength.

Simply persevere in expressing the truth of what you are; and the unmistakable force of invisible hands will ensure your eventual achievement. Envision your supreme calling and realize: *You can do it!*

> *"Until one is committed, there is hesitancy, the*
> *chance to draw back, always ineffectiveness.*
> *Concerning all acts of initiative (and creation),*
> *there is one elementary truth the ignorance of*
> *which kills countless ideas and splendid plans: that*
> *the moment one definitely commits oneself, then*
> *providence moves too. A whole stream of events*
> *issues from the decision, raising in one's favor all*
> *manner of unforeseen incidents, meetings and*
> *material assistance, which no man could have*
> *dreamt would have come his way ...*
> ***Whatever you can do***
> ***or dream you can,***
> ***begin it.***
> ***Boldness has genius,***
> ***power and magic in it!"***

~ W. H. Murray in The Scottish Himalaya
Expedition 1951, quoting Goethe (in bold).

Your Heart Will Sing

"GLORIA IN EXCELSIS DEO"

Your heart is the most exalted organ of your body. God speaks to you through your heart. When you give your heart authority in your life, it is a way of giving your life to God. When you surrender to your highest calling, your heart sings.

The song is sung differently by every heart, but the meaning is always the same. Each soul has their own special way of singing their heart's song.

Your heart's song is a reflection of your greatest purpose and your greatest contribution. When you are truly expressing your heart and soul, when you finally surrender to what you really are, your heart will be singing.

Others can sense when your heart is singing and are moved by it. They may not know why, but there is something different about you – something vibrant and beautiful.

When your heart sings it means you are offering your devotion to something bigger than your self. You are devoting yourself to the highest form of love and compassion available to you. You are no longer worshipping your own ego; you are worshiping the deep Truth that we all share.

Your heart comes alive when you are living your purpose.

Ask yourself at every turn, "What am I worshipping?"

From Punishment to Peace

Redemption occurs through surrendering the dualities of right or wrong, good or evil. These ideas are of the ego. Embrace the non-dualistic truth of your heart's will, which is impeccably obedient to God's Truth.

When you choose your heart, you are choosing The Great Will beyond your own smaller ego will. You are being lived through by Love. You are no longer making yourself in your own image; instead you are allowing Love to create through you – to shape you in the image of the divine.

This is Grace.

This is God's Music.

This is "It."

"Someday, after mastering the winds,
the waves, the tides and gravity,
we shall harness for God the energies of love,
and then, for a second time in the history of the
world, man will have discovered fire."
~ Pierre Teilhard de Chardin

Now express your fire and come alive. **It's time.**

A Special Invitation

Thank you for taking this extraordinary journey with us. You are among a distinguished group of fellow DaVincis who will transform our world in unimaginable ways. Because you've made it to the end of this book, you are clearly going to be one of the DaVinci success stories.

If you'd like to meet other DaVincis like yourself, please check out our online community at: **www.DaVinciMethod.com/club**

One of the best ways for you, as a DaVinci, to really learn something is to teach it and share it with others. You can help fellow DaVincis express themselves in this world as positive creators instead of succumbing to neurotic abuses. You can help them by inviting them to take this amazing journey too.

Our prisons are full of DaVinci types who never received the guidance they needed to become positive productive creators. The most destructive DaVincis are the ones who have most internalized the judgments of society for their spontaneous, impulsive, creative energy, taking on the identity of "the criminal" instead of "the Artist".

You can help troubled DaVincis regain their self-worth and their brilliance, by sharing the teachings of this book with them.

Who do you know who is also a DaVinci? The answer can't be far. If you're a DaVinci yourself, you are probably related to a few others.

We understand how important it is to make available The DaVinci Method to everyone who needs it, so we're giving you a special discount in order to help you spread the word. Use this link to get your special reader discount on additional copies of the DaVinci Method for friends and family:

www.DaVinciMethod.com/discount

How Has This Affected You?

We are deeply interested in your experiences with the teachings of The DaVinci Method. Please take a moment now to share with us your experience of this work.

Go here: **www.DaVinciMethod.com/feedback**

Spread the Fire ...

Would you like an easy way to share that charge you felt – when you realized you were a DaVinci – with other DaVincis who don't know it yet?

Watch this short inspirational web movie ...

www.AreYouaDaVinci.com

... and share it with those you know.

Appendix A: MENSA Riddles

The Light Bulb Problem:

Imagine you are outside a closed room with no windows and one door. You cannot see inside this room until you open the door.

There are three light switches in front of you. Each switch is connected to a different one of three light bulbs inside the closed room. All the light bulbs are currently off and thus all three switches are currently in the off position. You may flick on and off any of these switches as much as you like UNTIL you open the door and go inside the room to witness the state of the light bulbs. At that point you may no longer change the switches.

You may only open the door ONCE. THEN you must be able to tell which switch is connected to which light bulb.

In this scenario, how can you, with 100% certainty, tell which switch goes to which light bulb?

The Burning String Problem:

You have two lengths of string, which although they are not the same length, will each take exactly 30 minutes for a flame to burn from one end of the string to the other. The strings do not burn evenly, so the position of a flame, as it burns through a string, will not afford you any specific knowledge of how much time the string has been burning for. All you know is that it takes exactly 30 minutes for a flame to burn from one end of each string to the other end.

Without using a timepiece, how can you use these two strings and matches to measure out exactly 45 minutes with almost perfect accuracy?

ANSWERS on the next page …

MENSA Riddle Solutions

WARNING: Do not read these solutions until you've already got a solution. A good MENSA riddle can be hard to come by. You may even want to have a friend check your solution for you and just tell you if you're right or wrong, so you don't ruin it for yourself. The process of discovering the solution yourself is incredibly valuable.

The Light-bulb problem: I have seen this problem solved in two different ways ...

Solution 1: Turn on one switch (call it "switch one") and let it stay on for a while. Then turn that "switch one" off and turn on another switch (call it "switch two"). Open the door to the closed room and walk inside. The lit light bulb is obviously connected to "switch two". Now touch the two unlit light bulbs. The hot unlit light bulb is connected to "switch one". The cooler unlit light bulb is connected to the switch you never turned on.

Solution 2: Turn on one switch (call it "switch one") and let it stay on for a year. Then come back and turn on another switch (call it "switch two"). Open the door to the closed room and walk inside. The lit light bulb is obviously connected to "switch two". Now examine the two unlit light bulbs. The burned-out light bulb is connected to "switch one". The still fresh unlit light bulb is connected to the switch you never turned on.

The Burning String Problem: Light one of the strings aflame, not just on one end, but on both ends simultaneously. When the two flames reach each other (wherever along the string that may be), you will know you have measured out exactly 15 minutes. Immediately light one end of the other string and allow that to burn all the way through for the final 30 minutes. Voila! 45 minutes.

For more riddles visit: www.DaVinciMethod.com/mensa

Book Credits:

Will Therapy by Otto Rank

Truth and Reality by Otto Rank

The Ego and the Id by Sigmund Freud

The Interpretation of Dreams by Sigmund Freud

The Edison Gene by Thom Hartman

The Courage to Create by Rollo May

Understanding Yourself and Others by Linda V. Berens

Acting and the Unconscious by Eric Morris

Losing My Virginity by Richard Branson

Leonardo da Vinci Flights of the Mind by Charles Nicholl

Russell Bishop's forthcoming book

Success Principles by Jack Canfield

Bono: in conversation with Michka Assayas

Blink by Malcolm Gladwell

The Cashflow Quadrant by Robert T. Kiyosaki & Sharon Lechter

The Life of Leonardo da Vinci CBS 1972

The Artist's Way by Julia Cameron

Thom Hartman's Complete Guide to ADHD

Wholeness and the Implicate Order by David Bohm

Psychotherapy by Foundation for Inner Peace

ACIM by Foundation for Inner Peace

From Ego Self to True Self by Kenneth Wapnick

The Meme Machine by Susan Blackmore

The Future of the Body by Michael Murphy

The Hero with A Thousand Faces by Joseph Campbell

Endnotes:

---

[1] AMERICAN JOURNAL OF MEDICAL GENETICS (2003-08-15)

[2] 97. Seaman, M.I., Chang, F.M., Quinones, A.T. and Kidd, K.K. (2000)

Evolution of exon 1 of the dopamine D4 receptor (DRD4) gene in primates. J. Exp. Zool., 288, 32–38.

98. Ding, Y.C., Chi, H.C., Grady, D.L., Morishima, A., Kidd, J.R., Kidd, K.K., Flodman, P., Spence, M.A., Schuck, S., Swanson, J.M. et al.

(2002) Evidence of positive selection acting at the human dopamine receptor D4 gene locus. Proc. Natl Acad. Sci. USA, 99, 309–314.

[3] Human Molecular Genetics, 2004, Vol. 13, Review Issue 2

[4] http://www.ship.edu/~cgboeree/rank.html

[5] http://www.snr-jnt.org/JournalNT/JNT(2-3)4.html

[6] Biocybernaut Institute Santa Clara, California

[7] Biocybernaut Institute Santa Clara, California

8 From "EEG correlates of methylphenidate response among children with ADHD: a preliminary report" Sandra K. Loo , a, Peter D. Tealea and Martin L. Reitea

a Department of Psychiatry, University of Colorado Health Sciences Center, Denver, Colorado, USA

Received 2 March 1998; revised 20 July 1998; accepted 22 July 1998. Available online 11 June 1999.

[9] Kobayashi K, et al. 1998. Effects of L-theanine on the release of - brain waves in human volunteers. Nippon Noegik Kaishi 72:153-57.

[10] Brain Activity http://home.dmv.com/~tbastian/files/brain-wv.txt

[11] http://www.biofeedback1.com/add1.html

[12] Pg 149 Will Therapy by Otto Rank

[13] Adapted from a prayer found in A Course in Miracles

[14] p.154 Will Therapy by Otto Rank

[15] Pg 147 Will Therapy by Otto Rank

[16] Pg. 45 The Courage to Create, Rollo May, 1975

[17]http://www.lcc.ctc.edu/faculty/dmccarthy/engl204/seven-lecture.htm

[18] Adaptation of a passage from A Course in Miracles

[19] Story from Rollo May

[20]WebMuseum,   Paris   —
http://www.ibiblio.org/wm/paint/auth/vinci/

[21] What the @#$% do We Know?

00002B/121/P